The Palgrave Kets de Vries Library

Manfred F. R. Kets de Vries, Distinguished Professor of Leadership and Development and Organizational Change at INSEAD, is one of the world's leading thinkers on leadership, coaching, and the application of clinical psychology to individual and organizational change.

Palgrave's professional business list operates at the interface between academic rigor and real-world implementation. Professor Kets de Vries' work exemplifies that perfect combination of intellectual depth and practical application and Palgrave is proud to bring almost a decade's worth of work together in the Palgrave Kets de Vries Library.

More information about this series at
https://link.springer.com/bookseries/16661

Manfred F. R. Kets de Vries

The Daily Perils of Executive Life

How to Survive When Dancing on Quicksand

Manfred F. R. Kets de Vries
Paris, France

ISSN 2730-7581　　　　　　　ISSN 2730-759X　(electronic)
The Palgrave Kets de Vries Library
ISBN 978-3-030-91759-3　　　ISBN 978-3-030-91760-9　(eBook)
https://doi.org/10.1007/978-3-030-91760-9

© The Editor(s) (if applicable) and The Author(s), under exclusive licence to Springer Nature Switzerland AG 2022
This work is subject to copyright. All rights are solely and exclusively licensed by the Publisher, whether the whole or part of the material is concerned, specifically the rights of reprinting, reuse of illustrations, recitation, broadcasting, reproduction on microfilms or in any other physical way, and transmission or information storage and retrieval, electronic adaptation, computer software, or by similar or dissimilar methodology now known or hereafter developed.
The use of general descriptive names, registered names, trademarks, service marks, etc. in this publication does not imply, even in the absence of a specific statement, that such names are exempt from the relevant protective laws and regulations and therefore free for general use.
The publisher, the authors and the editors are safe to assume that the advice and information in this book are believed to be true and accurate at the date of publication. Neither the publisher nor the authors or the editors give a warranty, expressed or implied, with respect to the material contained herein or for any errors or omissions that may have been made. The publisher remains neutral with regard to jurisdictional claims in published maps and institutional affiliations.

This Palgrave Macmillan imprint is published by the registered company Springer Nature Switzerland AG.
The registered company address is: Gewerbestrasse 11, 6330 Cham, Switzerland.

Preface

I think we consider too much the good luck of the early bird and not enough the bad luck of the early worm. (Franklin D. Roosevelt)

A great man's greatest good luck is to die at the right time. (Erik Hoffer)

Recently, I was reminded the role the inconceivable plays in our lives. In early 2020 I delivered the first module of my long-running seminar for C-suite executives at INSEAD. Afterward, I told myself that it was the most effective module I could remember. But I'm given to pessimism, so almost immediately I found myself thinking, well, this can't last. It's all gone too seamlessly. There haven't been any hiccups. Something's bound to go wrong in the next module. And as the whole world learned soon enough, things went very wrong. There was no next module. If someone had told me that I would have to stop the workshop due to a pandemic, I would have rolled my eyes in disbelief. The idea would have been beyond even my deepest pessimism. Who would have thought that an incident supposedly taken place at a wet market in Wuhan would become the catalyst for a global pandemic? Reality can change its hue like a chameleon.

I should have known better. I have lived long enough to know that life's dice rolls in mysterious and random ways. The unimaginable is never far away and tragedy is always just round the corner. I remembered what happened to the Greek playwright Aeschylus, the father of dramatic tragedy. Legend has it that his personal ending was determined by the tragic convergence of three moveable objects: Aeschylus himself, a turtle, and a lammergeier, the bird also known as a bearded vulture.

Imagine a turtle. On this special day it wakes up hungry, as it does every morning, and crawls slowly toward some fresh green shoots. Unfortunately, its movements catch the eye of a lammergeier soaring high in the skies, also looking for breakfast; the bird sweeps down and grabs the reptile. But what now? As turtles do, it has withdrawn into its shell, making it difficult for the vulture to get at anything edible. But lammergeiers are no fools. The bird knows what to do next. Another of its names is ossifrage, or bone breaker. To be able to reach the marrow inside the large bones these vultures usually scavenge, they drop them from a great height, then glide down to inspect the results. They do this again and again until the bone is sufficiently cracked. Of course, this vulture did the same thing with the turtle. It dropped it, but instead of landing on a rock, the turtle landed on the skull of Aeschylus. According to this apocryphal story, the playwright spent most of his time outdoors. Ever since a prophecy had foretold that he would be killed by a falling object he had avoided manmade structures. What a tragic and absurd ending for the originator of tragedy. Fact can stretch our credulity even further than fiction.

But why a turtle? I am a psychoanalyst and in the habit of thinking about symbolism. Turtle symbolism is prevalent in many cultures. Often, the turtle symbolizes groundedness in moments of great disturbances and chaos. Turtles are closely tied to the earth—after all, they carry their home on their back—and move purposefully. They are symbols of stability, determination, endurance, wisdom, and long life. Anyway, as chance would have it, I found a turtle in my garden while self-isolating from the virus in the south of France. Where it came from still puzzles me although I'm sure it didn't fall from the sky. It appeared mysteriously and disappeared equally mysteriously. I hardly conjured it up but my interests in Aeschylus, turtles, and the pandemic are clearly tied together. It felt like joining the dots.

In a way we have all had a metaphorical turtle drop on to our head out of thin air, changing our lives dramatically. The pandemic came from nowhere and has been a rude awakening for all of us. It has showed us how fragile our planet is and how interconnected we are as human beings. The boundaries between our own problems and those of others have been largely erased. As the pandemic has forced us to change our behavior patterns, it has become a gigantic social experiment. We have all been moved out of our comfort zones and forced to change the way we deal with our lives. The cost of the pandemic has been terrible; as well as illness, it has been a time of mourning, with grief sharpened by survivors' separation from their loved ones when they died.

Like everyone else, the time since spring 2020 has been very strange for me. Like the turtle I found in my garden, I have single-mindedly pursued my personal antidote to the stress of confinement and focused on writing—a lot. This book is a collection of essays that are my personal attempts at sense-making. They reflect my concerns about the state of the world and many first saw the light of day serendipitously. Often, what I wrote was my reaction to current events, or responses to questions asked during the many podcasts and Zoom conferences in which I took part during lockdown.

I have divided this book into three sections. In the first section—Managing Self—I take a micro-perspective, reflecting on issues that we encounter in day-to-day living. The second section of the book—Leadership—takes more of an organizational perspective, while in the final section—Society—I look at larger social issues.

Writing entails periods of enforced solitude. It tends to be an introspective, contemplative activity, even approaching an altered state of consciousness. By its very nature, writing is an encounter with your personal muse—an exploratory journey into the unknown frontiers of your self. In fact, when you're alone with yourself for extended periods of time, trying to write down your thoughts, you learn a lot about yourself. Therefore, writing can be transformational.

To me, writing is a form of refined thinking in that it forces me to turn my thoughts inward, to discover things within myself and in the world around me, things I otherwise wouldn't have noticed. And I know that how I think and create my inner world affects what I become in my outer world. Writing has always helped me understand what really matters to me. Often, I don't really know what I think about something until I read what I have written about it. In other words, writing has always helped me to own my own story. In that respect, in the context of my long educational journey to becoming a psychoanalyst, writing is a continuation of my therapeutic training.

Furthermore, writing has always been my way of exploring what I don't know, or to be more precise, what I don't know yet but would like to know. It has helped me to explore, uncover and investigate the mysteries of human nature. I have come to realize that taking such a journey isn't effortless but at the same time, I know that I write because it is difficult. Often, leaving my comfort zone can be gut-wrenching. It impacts otherwise unexplored parts of my brain. In that respect, writing shapes character, making me appreciate the things that are worth doing.

Another motivation to write comes from my urge to share my words, thoughts, and passions with the world. I'm aware that this might sound rather narcissistic, but my fantasy has always been that if something matters to me, who knows, it may also matter to other people. And I persist in doing so, because I believe strongly that all of us should engage in things that are bigger than ourselves. The mythologist Joseph Campbell wrote, "When we quit thinking primarily about ourselves and our own self-preservation, we undergo a truly heroic transformation of consciousness." In that respect, writing is the concretization of my ideas; it gives my ideas substance and allows them to travel. And I hope, through the spread of these ideas, that I might effect change, for the better. As I have discovered for myself, reading what people have written can change lives. After all, if we don't change, we don't grow. And it we don't grow, we aren't really living.

Anyone who has tried to write knows that writing can be an extremely lonely affair. Fortunately, my efforts at writing don't take place in a complete vacuum. There are several people I have always been able to lean on. I am very grateful to David Champion, senior editor of the *Harvard Business Review*, who has always been extremely encouraging in helping me turn my ideas into reality. In particular, he has always pushed me to reflect on recommendations for action when writing for the *Review*, something that doesn't always come easily as many of the problems I deal with professionally don't lend themselves to straightforward answers. I also want to thank Isabelle Laporte, senior editor of *INSEAD Knowledge*, for her encouraging positivity. Isabelle taught me how to restructure my texts more succinctly. In particular, I am also extremely grateful for the editorial help of my long-time editor, Sally Simmons, a real editor's editor. The many books I have written would never have seen the light of day without her input. In addition, my collaborator, Alicia Cheak-Baillargeon, has always been remarkable for her speed in responding to my editorial queries. Of course, there is also my cheerleader, Elisabet Engellau, always prepared, in her very subtle way, to give me constructive feedback.

Paris, France   Manfred F. R. Kets de Vries

Contents

Part I	Managing Self	1
1	What Do the Five Pillars of Meaning Mean to You?	3
2	How Do You Rate on Your Energy Barometer?	7
3	Are You Creating "Eureka Moments"?	11
4	Is Revenge a Dish Best Not Served at All?	15
5	How to Cultivate Patience in an Impatient World	19
	Flexing the Patience "Muscle"	21
	Discover Your Patience Triggers	21
	Reframe the Situation	22
	Fantasize	22
	Practice Empathy	22
	Practice Gratitude	23
	Use Humor	23
	Be Realistic	23
	Practice Mindfulness	24
	Ask Others for Help	24
6	Groundhog Day: A Learning Experience	25

7	**The Labyrinth of Forgetfulness**	29
	The Neural Circuit	30
	The Role of Novelty	31
	Cognitive Illusions	32
	Managing Our Time	32
8	**The Triumph of Hope over Experience**	35
	Lesson 1: Making the Right Choice	36
	Lesson 2: Why Marry?	37
	Lesson 3: Fear of Ending up Alone	37
	Lesson 4: Unfinished Business	38
	Lesson 5: Mutual Respect	39
	Lesson 6: Trust	39
	Lesson 7: Forgiveness	40
	Lesson 8: Communication	40
	Lesson 9: Space	41
	Lesson 10: Growing Together	41

Part II   Leadership   45

9	How Is Your Shadow Side Treating You?	47
10	Everything Is Bad: Complaining as a Way of Life	51
11	The Belligerent (B) Personality	55
12	Managing "On the Borderline"	61
13	How to Support People Struggling with Poor Mental Health?	69
14	What Is This Person Really Telling Me?	75
15	Are You Working in a Trust-Based Organization?	81
16	Co-leadership: A Curse or a Blessing?	85
17	Onboarding or Unboarding?	91

Part III	Society	97
18	Is Democracy in the Workplace a Mirage?	99
19	The Societal Costs of Loneliness	105
20	Bluebeard Revisited	111
21	Do We Get the Leaders We Deserve?	115
22	Why Do Societies Regress?	119
23	Drinking the Kool-Aid	123
Epilogue		129
Index		133

About the Author

Manfred Florian Kets de Vries brings a different view to the much-studied subjects of leadership and the psychological dimensions of individual and organizational change. Bringing to bear his knowledge and experience of economics (Econ. Drs., University of Amsterdam), management (ITP, MBA, and DBA, Harvard Business School), and psychoanalysis (Membership Canadian Psychoanalytic Society, Paris Psychoanalytic Society, and the International Psychoanalytic Association), he explores the interface between management science, psychoanalysis, developmental psychology, evolutionary psychology, neuroscience, psychotherapy, executive coaching, and consulting. His specific areas of interest are leadership (the "bright" and "dark" side), entrepreneurship, career dynamics, talent management, family business, cross-cultural management, succession planning, organizational and individual stress, C-suite team building, executive coaching, organizational development, transformation management, and management consulting.

The Distinguished Clinical Professor of Leadership Development and Organizational Change at INSEAD, he is Program Director of INSEAD's top management program, "The Challenge of Leadership: Creating Reflective Leaders," and the Founder of INSEAD's Executive Master Program in Change Management. As an educator, he has received INSEAD's distinguished teacher award six times. He has held professorships at McGill University; the École des Hautes Études Commerciales, Montreal; the European School for Management and Technology (ESMT), Berlin; and the Harvard Business School. He has lectured at management institutions around the world. *The Financial Times*, *Le Capital*, *Wirtschaftswoche*, and *The Economist* have rated Manfred Kets de Vries among the world's leading management thinkers and among the most influential contributors to human resource management.

Kets de Vries is the author, co-author, or editor of more than fifty books, including *The Neurotic Organization, Leaders, Fools and Impostors, Life and Death in the Executive Fast Lane, The Leadership Mystique, The Happiness Equation, Are Leaders Born or Are They Made? The Case of Alexander the Great, The New Russian Business Elite, Lessons on Leadership by Terror: Finding Shaka Zulu in the Attic, The Global Executive Leadership Inventory, The Leader on the Couch, Coach and Couch, Family Business on the Couch, Sex, Money, Happiness, and Death: The Quest for Authenticity, Reflections on Character and Leadership, Reflections on Leadership and Career Development, Reflections on Groups and Organizations, The Coaching Kaleidoscope, The Hedgehog Effect: The Secrets of Building High Performance Teams, Mindful Leadership Coaching: Journeys into the Interior, You Will Meet a Tall Dark Stranger: Executive Coaching Challenges, Telling Fairy Tales in the Boardroom: How to Make Sure Your Organization Lives Happily Ever After, Riding the Leadership Roller Coaster: An Observer's Guide, Down the Rabbit Hole of Leadership: Leadership Pathology in Everyday Life, Journeys into Coronavirus Land: Lessons from a Pandemic, The CEO Whisperer: Meditations on Leadership, Life and Change, Quo Vadis?: The Existential Challenges of Leaders, Leadership Unhinged: Essays on the Ugly, the Bad, and the Weird*, and *Leading Wisely: Becoming a Reflective Leader in Turbulent Times*.

In addition, Kets de Vries has published more than four hundred academic papers as chapters in books and as articles. He has also written more than a hundred case studies, including seven that received the Best Case of the Year award. He is a regular writer for various magazines. Furthermore, his work has been featured in such publications as *The New York Times, The Wall Street Journal, The Los Angeles Times, Fortune, Business Week, The Economist, The Financial Times*, and *The Harvard Business Review*. His books and articles have been translated into more than thirty languages. He has written more than a hundred blogs (mini articles) for the *Harvard Business Review* and *INSEAD Knowledge*. He is a member of seventeen editorial boards and is a Fellow of the Academy of Management. He is also a founding member of the International Society for the Psychoanalytic Study of Organizations (ISPSO), which has honored him as a lifetime member. Kets de Vries is also the first non-US recipient of International Leadership Association Lifetime Achievement Award for his contributions to leadership research and development (being considered one of the world's founding professionals in the development of leadership as a field and discipline). In addition, he received a Lifetime Achievement Award from Germany for his advancement of executive education. The American Psychological Association has honored him with the "Harry and Miriam Levinson Award" for his contributions to Organizational Consultation. Furthermore, he is the recipient of the "Freud Memorial

Award" for his work to further the interface between management and psychoanalysis. In addition, he has also received the "Vision of Excellence Award" from the Harvard Institute of Coaching. Kets de Vries is the first beneficiary of INSEAD's Dominique Héau Award for "Inspiring Educational Excellence." He is also the recipient of two honorary doctorates. The Dutch government has made him an Officer in the Order of Oranje Nassau.

Kets de Vries works as a consultant on organizational design/transformation and strategic human resource management for companies worldwide. As an educator and consultant, he has worked in more than forty countries. In his role as a consultant, he is also the founder-chairman of the Kets de Vries Institute (KDVI), a boutique strategic leadership development consulting firm.

Kets de Vries was the first fly fisherman in Outer Mongolia (at the time, becoming the world record holder of the Siberian hucho taimen). He is a member of New York's Explorers Club. In his spare time, he can be found in the rainforests or savannas of Central and Southern Africa, the Siberian taiga, the Ussuri Krai, Kamchatka, the Pamir and Altai Mountains, Arnhemland, or within the Arctic Circle.

Part I

Managing Self

1

What Do the Five Pillars of Meaning Mean to You?

> *Begin at once to live, and count each day as a separate life.*
> —*Seneca*
>
> *Our prime purpose in this life is to help others. And if you can't help them, at least don't hurt them.*
> —*The Dalai Lama*

Paul, one of the executives participating in the C-suite seminar at INSEAD that I have been running for a very long time, wanted to talk to me. He confided that he had enrolled in my program because he was feeling lost. Having taken a long, hard look at his life, everything seemed meaningless. On the surface, he appeared to be a very successful businessman, but his achievements no longer gave him satisfaction. What he felt instead was boredom—and dread.

I asked Paul to think about any recurring patterns in his life. His reply was that he had always been a one-trick pony. There had never been much else in his life apart from work. After some prompting from me, he joined the dots and began to see how his workaholism had affected his interpersonal relationships. He had plenty of business acquaintances but no real friends. His relationships with close family members were perfunctory. He realized that he had always taken his wife and children for granted. For some time now, his wife had been doing her own thing. They had become like two people who were just sharing accommodation, with very little connection between them. When I asked Paul if he had ever dreamt of an alternative career, he said that he would have loved to be an orchestra conductor but that his father had scotched that idea.

Listening to Paul reminded me of a poignant observation made by Victor Frankl, Holocaust survivor and psychiatrist: "Ever more people today have the means to live, but no meaning to live for."[1] Sadly, Paul's story is not unusual. I have heard many variations on his theme during my workshops, with the only differences in the detail. Many program participants—highly successful men and women in top-level posts in top-level organizations—struggle with what I call the five pillars of meaning: belonging, purpose, competence, control, and transcendence.[2]

At the core of humankind's search for meaning is our awareness that our stay on earth is limited. A major driving force in the search for meaning is death anxiety.[3] As a "stealth motivator," death can propel us to make the best of our life experience. In Paul's case, getting older might have been the catalyst that made meaning top of mind for him. At a certain point in life, we must let go of our youthful illusion of immortality and transition from "time to live" to "time left to live," and with that comes a new sense of urgency. For many of us, however, accepting that at some point we are no longer going to be here remains incomprehensible.

Let's take a closer look at these five pillars of meaning. To start with, meaning is anchored in our sense of *belonging*—our need for affectionate interpersonal relationships, to bond with others and not to feel alone. However, many people underestimate the importance of social ties as protection as they deal with the vicissitudes of life. Every interaction we have with others, whether it brings joy, disgust, anger, or sadness, allows us to learn more about who we are and what we want. But when we are supported by others through such experiences and challenges, we cope much more effectively.[4] All too often, however, people build walls instead of bridges. It's clear from Paul's story that he did not invest enough in this extremely important part of his life.

Meaning is also tied to the extent to which we can find *purpose*, which is integral to activities and interests. It is a future-oriented activity that give us a sense of direction, energizes us and drives us toward action. People with a

---

[1] Victor Frankl (2006). *Man's Search for Meaning*. Boston: Beacon Press.
[2] Manfred F. R. Kets de Vries (2021). *Quo Vadis: The Existential Challenges of Leaders*. London: Palgrave Macmillan.
[3] Irvin D. Yalom (2009). *Staring at the Sun: Overcoming the Terror of Death.* San Francisco: Jossey-Bass; Manfred F. R. Kets de Vries (2014). Death and the executive: Encounters with the "Stealth" motivator, *Organizational Dynamics*, 43 (4), 247–256.
[4] George Vaillant (2008). *Aging Well: Surprising Guideposts to a Happier Life from the Landmark Study of Adult Development*. Boston: Little Brown & Company.

clear picture of what they want to do tend to be those who thrive in life. In comparison, people with no clear sense of purpose merely exist and find little meaning in whatever they're doing. Even though Paul believed he found purpose through the creation of several companies, the work that he looked forward to had now lost its meaningfulness.

The third pillar of meaning, *competence*, is tied to our sense of self-efficacy, or how we use and master our unique talents. It is also linked to confidence in our own abilities, specifically in our ability to meet challenges and complete successfully the activities we undertake. High levels of competence often involve being "in the zone," being completely immersed in whatever we're doing. Even though Paul's deep-down wish had been to become a successful orchestral conductor, he also had a talent for business, which he pursued and for some time found enjoyable.

The fourth pillar—*control*—we tend to take for granted. It refers to the degree to which we believe we have freedom of choice and freedom to take personal responsibility for the choices we make. Some of the more important choices we make are of partner and career and both were troubling Paul when we had our conversation. Had he chosen his wife under societal pressure rather than from deep personal conviction? Looking back, did he get married because it seemed everybody else his age was already married? And of course, as far as his career was concerned, entrepreneurship was a definite second option behind music.

The final pillar or meaning is *transcendence*, how we connect ourselves to issues larger than ourselves and contribute purposefully to our community and society at large. Transcendence has to do with our willingness to move beyond self-interest and self-fulfilment by making room within ourselves for others. As a Greek proverb puts it, "society grows great when old men plant trees whose shade they know they shall never sit in." Transcendence, however, had never been part of Paul's life—he had been too obsessed with making his companies successful to think about planting metaphorical trees.

Paul had taken me into his confidence, and I wondered how I could draw on these five pillars of meaning to help him build a sense of meaning and direction at this crossroads in his life. Should I suggest that he focus on his relationship with his wife and children? Or was it already too late? Given his undeniable financial security, should he devote his time to music, his original passion? Should he become a patron of the arts, tapping into his passion while transcending personal concerns by investing in the passions of others? If he made these changes, would Paul acquire a greater sense of purpose and control over his life?

Moments of existential crisis, like Paul's, can be great learning opportunities. The novelist Herman Hesse wrote: "I have always believed, and I still believe, that whatever good or bad fortune may come our way we can always give it meaning and transform it into something of value." Overcoming challenges can make life more meaningful. I was hopeful for Paul: he still had many options open to explore new things and gain a sense of meaningful direction. The choice, however, would be up to him.

2

How Do You Rate on Your Energy Barometer?

The energy of the mind is the essence of life.
—*Aristotle*
And what is a man without energy? Nothing—nothing at all.
—*Mark Twain*

"Dirk, what's happening to you? Why do you look so down? Is something wrong?" I was talking to the CEO of a bank, whom I knew quite well, and who, after a short silence, replied with an avalanche of words. Clearly, he needed to get a lot off his chest. He told me that he has been feeling exhausted for some time. When I asked about his work, he said he got very little pleasure from it—too many meetings, most of them with people he didn't like, but given his position in the company he couldn't really get out of them. Masquerading as a positive person tired him out. His insomnia didn't help. When he did fall asleep, he had bad dreams, which made him wonder what his brain was trying to tell him. In his own words, "sometimes the worst place you can be is in your own head." Clearly, Dirk wasn't in good mental shape.

I asked Dirk if he kept a diary or a similar record of his daily activities. Suppose he identified the activities that energized him and the ones that drained him? His annotations would reveal the situations when he felt he was (or wasn't) at his best. He might even be able to identify salient positive and negative themes using this personal "energy barometer." Awareness of situations and activities that affected him negatively would help him find ways to preempt them.

My encounter with Dirk got me thinking about the general question of bad habits. All of us can fall into bad habits. The question is whether we recognize them and whether we do something about them. I decided to ask the executives participating in my yearly C-suite seminar at INSEAD what kinds of bad habits they had and whether they had a negative effect on their mental health. The list was an interesting one.

I wasn't surprised that top of the list came *addiction to the Internet*. And although the endless stream of communications would stress them out, but they also admitted to spending a considerable amount of time surfing the net and getting distracted from their primary tasks. Similarly, some mentioned that they were spending a lot of time *looking at television or streaming services*, and talked about the negative effects of watching violent or scary movies. These activities took up an enormous amount of their time and energy, often at the cost of more energizing activities, such as spending time with family and friends.

Another negative effect was the very little energy left for more *creative endeavors*. For example, reading—an activity that impacts the brain both psychologically and neurologically, boosting its capacity for empathy—fell by the wayside. Their Internet addiction also meant they spent little time *exercising and being outdoors*. Although they knew the benefits of exercise and exposure to nature for both their physical and mental health, there were few occasions when they took the time.

Another bad habit was *hurry sickness*. Many admitted that their workload (including excessive travel) meant they felt and behaved like the rabbit in *Alice's Adventures in Wonderland*, frantic that time was running out. They acknowledged that this state of mind could be exhausting.

This discussion led to several executives talking about their ineffectiveness in *setting priorities and boundaries*. Interestingly, while some of them complained about a *lack of structure*, others complained that their lives were *overstructured*—giving them very little freedom to pursue energizing activities.

Some executives added that they often felt *they didn't own their own life*. They felt they were *trying to please everybody* and living their lives *according to other people's prescriptions*. The effort of trying to please everybody left them with stress, anxiety, and depressive feelings.

Many admitted they had also gotten into *poor eating habits*. They ate too much fast food or ate excessively as a form of antidepressant. Several had serious weight problems. Others told me that, as a way of numbing the emotional labor required of them, they *self-medicated* with excessive drinking and drugs.

A common marker on the energy barometer was *having to deal with negative people*. Some participants talked about playing the role of "garbage can," and how the most negative people were also often the most difficult to avoid, like bosses or family members. This observation led to a discussion about why some of them *stayed too long in unhappy relationships*. Although these were immense energy drainers, they often didn't know how to get out of them.

Making this spontaneous list of bad habits encouraged some frank exchanges. For example, several executives admitted that they resorted to many of their energy draining activities to *avoid the big issues* in their lives. This is known as the "manic defense," a behavior pattern whereby people try to distract their conscious mind from uncomfortable and unpleasant thoughts with either a flurry of activities or opposing thoughts or feelings. Fearing introspection, they tend to pack unpleasant issues away in their unconscious, not wanting to look at them. Unfortunately, these issues tend to pop up unexpectedly in uglier, more energy-draining ways.

This discussion brought participants to the theme of *perfectionism*—of setting extremely high standards for themselves. Many of them seemed to be very hard on themselves, unable to accept that it is OK not to be perfect and that making mistakes is a pathway to further growth and development. Some of them seemed to be intent on tormenting themselves, stressing over things they couldn't control. Their level of perfectionism turned out to be a true energy drainer.

I was left with the thought that we should all know what our "energy barometer" looks like. Thus, if any of these issues resonate with you, what are you doing about it? How could you restructure your life to focus on activities that add value and vigor and avoid activities that drain you of energy? As we so often discover, the Greeks got there long before any of us. For example, Aristotle identified two elements of a fulfilling life: *eudaimonia*, happiness gained by living virtuously, and *hedonia*, the pursuit of subjective well-being, the fundamental pleasures afforded by food, sex, and social interactions.

With these thoughts in mind, I wondered how I could be helpful to Dirk, and other executives, who struggle with a lack of well-being and happiness. What suggestions could I make to help them improve their mental health? My immediate thought was "oxygen masks." We are told that if a plane is in trouble we should put on our own oxygen mask first, before helping others with theirs. Applying this to personal energy and physical and mental health, we need to take care of ourselves before we can take care of other people. Self-care is an essential first step to help Dirk and others feel better in their skin.

Self-sacrifice, and always putting on a brave face is not the way to go. There is nothing weak about being less than perfect and asking for help. In fact, Dirk's openness about his unhappiness was a very courageous first step. When he took an honest look at his life, he discovered that the biggest energy drainer was trying to live according to others' expectations while denying his own. It made him decide that the pressure was dangerously high on his own energy barometer. It was time to change his behavior.

3

Are You Creating "Eureka Moments"?

Eureka! (I have found it!)
—Archimedes
I have no special talent. I am only passionately curious.
—Albert Einstein

Many years ago, I was asked by the CEO of a conglomerate to sit in on one of their executive meetings to observe their team dynamics. What surprised me during the meeting was that they spent a remarkable amount of time discussing various issues, but that no decisions were made. When I commented on this to the CEO, he said, "The decisions are for tomorrow." When I asked why, he replied that he had discovered that the quality of decisions was so much better when everyone had the chance to have a good night's sleep. According to him, sleep helped them to see complex problems in a very different light. It seemed he wanted to turn the problem over to his executives' unconscious mind—to let it work while they were sleeping.

This comment made me think of the story of Archimedes, perhaps the greatest scientist of antiquity, and the original "eureka moment." According to historical records, the King of Syracuse suspected that a goldsmith commissioned to make him a crown had cheated by mixing silver with the gold and asked Archimedes to find a way to prove it. For a while, Archimedes was stumped; short of melting the crown down (not an option) there was no existing method to test the purity of the metal. The story goes that, taking a bath, Archimedes noticed that the level of the water increased the more of him got in it. He realized that if he put a lump of pure gold, weighing the exact weight of the crown, in water and measured how much water was displaced, he would know what the density of the crown should be. If the actual crown displaced less water, he would know that less valuable material had been used to make it. Archimedes was allegedly so excited by his solution that he jumped out of his bath and ran naked through the streets, shouting "Eureka!"—or "I have found it!"

Both my CEO and Archimedes found a creative solution after a period of incubation, an often ignored but critical process in finding solutions to knotty problems. Over and over again, stories of scientific breakthroughs and artistic triumphs show that putting a problem aside, not thinking about it consciously and letting the brain operate busily behind the scenes for a while, helps fuel creative thought processes. This is often referred to as the "three Bs" of creativity: that is, great ideas may pop up while we are in bed, in the bath, or on the bus—in other words, when our mind is temporarily diverted from a problem. Haven't we all experienced situations when we have spent an enormous amount of time and energy thinking about a problem, only to have the solution pop into consciousness out of the blue, typically while we are traveling, on waking up, or taking a shower? It might just be a crossword solution—we can't all be Archimedes—but it might equally well be a genuinely tricky personal or professional problem. Both show the value of letting our mind wander, of daydreaming and dreaming, allowing our unconscious to work undisturbed.

In today's world of continuous change, we need the contributions of creative individuals more than ever. Creativity plays an overriding role in many areas of our life—in education, the arts, science, and the economy in general. I am not just referring to creativity with a capital C, finding the Higgs boson or a Banksy work of social commentary; I'm also thinking of creativity with a small c, the more humdrum insights that solve knotty problems on a day-to-day basis.

Many creative ideas do indeed seem to emerge after they have been slept on. For example, Paul McCartney recalled dreaming his song "Yesterday" and waking up with it fully written in his head. Famously, the scientist August Kekulé dreamt about a self-devouring snake and woke up realizing he had uncovered the ring structure of benzene.

There are two broad categories of sleep: rapid eye movement (REM) sleep and non-rapid-eye-movement (NREM) sleep. Our mental activity during NREM sleep is believed to be comparable to conscious thought, whereas our REM sleep includes more hallucinatory and puzzling imagery. It appears that cognition during REM sleep is qualitatively quite different from that of waking and NREM sleep. The dreams we recall most vividly usually occur during

REM sleep, reflecting a shift in the associative memory system. This shift in cognitive processing may be responsible for the bizarre nature of many dreams. It facilitates connectivity, however, between weakly associated memories—a process that enhances creative thinking. Due to the unconscious recombination of elements of thought, REM sleep is highly conducive to fluid reasoning and flexible thinking.

Advances in neuroscience have provided additional evidence of the mechanisms underlying this incubation effect, especially during sleep. Using functional magnetic resonance imaging (fMRI), scientists can understand what happens, and how, when our mind wanders, detecting greater activity in the brain's frontal and parietal cortex that generates creative ideas and novel associations.

Given what we know about the importance of incubation, what can we do to improve our creative thought processes?

The Dutch have a straightforward term, *niksen*, which means doing nothing, being completely idle, or doing something of no use at all. While meditative practices can feel like yet another thing to do, *niksen* is so much simpler. It is the antithesis of mindfulness, which requires us to pay attention to every single passing thought and sensation. It has nothing to do with transcendental meditation, which involves concentrating on our breathing and chanting mantras. The whole point of *niksen* is that it is purposeless. It can be as simple as just hanging around, looking out of the window, lying on the sofa, or listening to music—as long as we're not doing it for any reason. *Niksen* is about letting our mind wander without thinking about doing things. Our brain will still be processing information and trying to solve problems. And *niksen* is a great context for eureka moments. Just don't expect them to happen immediately. The unconscious mind needs to be given enough time to wander, to pursue fantasies, and assimilate information gathered from diverse sources. We cannot force the process. It can take days, weeks, or even years before it happens. Michelangelo walked round the block of marble that would eventually become his *David* for a month before he picked up a chisel and made the first cut.

When I work with executives who are "stuck," in one way or another, I always suggest that they take a break and do something very different from the main task at hand. I tell them that it is important to step back from the problem. They should focus their conscious mind on something completely separate from the problem that needs solving. Doing nothing, sleeping on it, or finding other distractions will help bring about their own eureka moment. They usually need some convincing, as doing nothing is anathema to them. Many find it difficult to let go of the busyness of conscious thought.

Unfortunately, unrelenting busyness is an obstacle rather than an accomplishment. As I discussed in Chap. 2, the manic defense of constant engagement can be counterproductive.

However, rest and leisure can be highly productive, thanks to the power of our unconscious mind. When we engage in activities that make us relaxed and happy, dopamine—the neurotransmitter that helps our mind to wander and activates the creative process—is released in the brain. It is up to each of us to find the best way of stimulating this creative time out. There is no one-size-fits-all approach. For some, it might be solitude; for others it might be time spent with friends and family. The important thing is to do something completely different. A good example is Albert Einstein, who reckoned he came up with some of his best ideas while he was playing the violin.

I should add that creative solutions don't come out of nowhere. We need first to immerse ourselves in a problem before letting go of it and allowing time and space for unconscious processing. Stimulating the creative process is a very delicate dance. As the actor and comedian John Cleese put it: "Your creativity acts like a tortoise—poking its head out nervously to see if the environment is safe before it fully emerges. Thus, you need to create a tortoise enclosure—an oasis amongst the craziness of modern life—to be a safe haven where your creativity can emerge."

4

Is Revenge a Dish Best Not Served at All?

> *The best revenge is not to be like your enemy.*
> —Marcus Aurelius
>
> *…[B]ut I, who have also been betrayed, assassinated and cast into a tomb, I have emerged from that tomb by the grace of God and I owe it to God to take my revenge. He has sent me for that purpose. Here I am.*
> —Alexandre Dumas

Many of us have read the classic novel *The Count of Monte Cristo* by the French author Alexandre Dumas. It is the story of Edmond Dantès, a simple, honorable sailor, who is betrayed by people he thinks are his friends but turn out to be envious of his accomplishments. One of them is his best friend, who is after Dantès' girlfriend. Framed for an offence he did not commit, Dantès is imprisoned for life on the island of Chateau d'If. He is there for fourteen years, spending every waking moment obsessed with the idea of revenge, before he escapes with the help of another prisoner. Once free, Dantès reinvents himself as the hugely wealthy Count of Monte Cristo—the first step in his plan to exact revenge on those responsible for his imprisonment.

As the novel progresses, we see how Dantès' plans for revenge have devastating consequences for both the innocent and the guilty, making it a story not only about revenge but also about the limitations of human justice. When it was published in 1846 (and for some time afterward), *The Count of Monte Cristo* became the most popular book in Europe. It appeared that everyone could identify with Dantès. The thirst for vengeance—the *lex talionis*, an eye for an eye—is a timeless theme that most of us can relate to.

Many of us know exactly what injustice feels like and have had to deal with being manipulated by the forces of unreasonable power. Many of us have had experiences that left us feeling misunderstood or cheated and longing to get even. It is a universal reaction. But even if we don't experience it ourselves, we see in real life, fiction, and all types of entertainment that people are falsely accused of wrongdoing by envious friends or subject to anonymous denunciations. Revenge is the single explanation for motive in innumerable TV dramas and movie sagas. And we all see how often the "bad guys" go unpunished. Dantès, however, turns revenge into a sustained creative project and makes a high art out of giving people their just deserts.

The popularity of Dumas' novel, first serialized over a period of two years, was assured from the start. But although it is primarily a story of revenge, *The Count of Monte Cristo* becomes much more as the novel develops. Dantès finds the revenge he spent fourteen years planning and perfecting less satisfying than he had hoped for. Revenge neither heals his wounds nor brings redemption. He finds reconciliation with his fate and ultimate peace in a very different quarter. This leaves us with the question whether we should follow Dantès' example when we feel like taking revenge. Is tit-for-tat the way to go? Does taking revenge really make us feel better? Or is it true, as Dantès finds, that vengeance is not good for the soul and in fact brings out the worst in us?

Maybe we should start to answer these questions by asking ourselves another. Why does revenge play such an important role in our psyche? Has it perhaps been imprinted in us? From an evolutionary point of view, it is arguable that revenge has always played an important role in keeping societies working smoothly. In a somewhat contorted way, the threat of revenge can be a protective mechanism, a kind of enforcement of social cooperation and justice. The possibility of revenge deters transgression of the social contract. From this perspective, we can hypothesize that our Paleolithic ancestors used revenge to enforce the rule that every individual must pull his or her weight in cooperative efforts (such as hunting or defending the group as a whole). The threat of revenge would have reinforced collaboration and prevented free riding.

From a more psychological perspective, it could be argued that while revenge doesn't undo the harm that's been done, it can restore the balance of suffering between the victim and the transgressor. In exacting revenge, victims of perceived injustice can restore their sense of self-worth and self-esteem by demonstrating that nobody can walk over them.

But while the *idea* of revenge—imagining the various ways in which we might get back at the person who has done us wrong—provides a delectable sense of satisfaction, revenge itself is rarely sweet and the feelings it produces are rarely unmixed. If revenge is a dish best served cold, wouldn't it be better to forget all about it once it has become so unappetizing? After all, it can leave a very bitter aftertaste. The difficult part of revenge is living afterward with the action taken. Revenge only ever feels sweet when the transgressor recognizes and accepts that he or she has done harm.

I am making this point because people preoccupied by revenge are more likely to suffer from a variety of adverse psychological and physiological disorders, including greater negative affect and depression, as well as reduced life satisfaction.[1] Ironically, revenge can prolong the distress of the original offense, while the actual execution of revenge can carry a high cost in terms of time, and emotional and physical energy. Taken to the extreme of legitimate or illegitimate justice, it can even lead to the loss of life.

There are a couple of caveats to be made here. First, in societies where legal and institutional rules are weak, or in subcultures where victims cannot rely on the legal system, personal revenge is often the only means available for restoring justice and honor. Second, people with specific personality profiles are more likely to act violently when they feel wronged. For example, people with narcissistic or antisocial (psychopathic) personality characteristics will be hellbent on revenge due to their sense of entitlement and vengeful disposition. Not only will they feel fewer constraints, but they may also find destroying other people's lives remarkably cathartic.

Keeping these caveats in mind, generally speaking people eager for revenge may be "digging two graves," as a Chinese proverb puts it—"one for your enemy, and one for yourself." Revenge will not bring back what we have lost. Indeed, revenge often provokes revenge, which provokes further revenge, and so on—an endless chain of pain and destruction in which the score is never evened.

In one way, revenge can be seen as a perverse form of reparatory communication. Once it is enacted, we may even feel inferior to our target, making revenge a self-defeating exercise. The paradox of vengefulness is that it makes us dependent on those who have done us harm, believing that our release from pain will come only when we make our tormentors suffer. The great danger is that when we repay evil with evil, we may become evil ourselves. It is much better, both morally and for our mental and physical health, to bin the cold and rancid dish of revenge and get on with life. Better perhaps, but not necessarily easy. Forgiving and forgetting requires strength, conserving the energy that would otherwise be wasted on the feelings and actions of revenge

---

[1] https://greatergood.berkeley.edu/images/uploads/McCullough-Dispositional_Vengefulness_Correlates.pdf.

that will ultimately diminish our self-respect. As someone once said, not forgiving is like drinking rat poison and then waiting for the rat to die. There is tremendous beauty in the unintended revenge of living well and being happy. According to the philosopher-king Roman Emperor Marcus Aurelius, "The best revenge is to be unlike him who performed the injury." In other words, the best revenge is true forgiveness.

I touched earlier on the satisfaction our fantasies of revenge can bring. Perhaps, while fantasizing, we could also think about the consequences of our fantasies if we acted them out. The reality is that acts of revenge do not really bring reparation and a sense of justice. It's much wiser to calm down and reflect on the alternatives before making any rash decisions. If we believe that we have been treated badly—if we feel a sense of injustice—we should also ask ourselves whether we are sure we have all the facts. What really happened—and why—might be quite different from our perception of events. When we act vengefully, there is a significant chance that we will create more suffering for ourselves and others and regret our actions later. Indeed, Edmond Dantès has the bitterness of realizing this himself after his long project of revenge: "'Fool that I am,' said he, 'that I did not tear out my heart the day I resolved to revenge myself!'"

5

How to Cultivate Patience in an Impatient World

Patience is a conquering virtue.
—Geoffrey Chaucer
Patience is bitter, but its fruit is sweet.
—Jean-Jacques Rousseau

The whole world had been waiting for something to happen—the "something" being a vaccine against the coronavirus. Without a vaccine, life could never return to normal. Since its almost miraculous arrival, we have come to realize that it has been a game changer. However, while we were waiting for it, we were all like the characters in Samuel Becket's play *Waiting for Godot*. Unlike the play, however, in which it's clear that Godot will never come, in our case, something did. A "cure" for the virus has been found but until the vaccine is available to everyone, we will still need to be patient, which is difficult when we are dealing with an invisible enemy that's causing so much misery to so many.

It's been difficult to remain cool, calm, and collected in the context of the pandemic. Covid-19 has transformed our lives dramatically—and not necessarily for the better.[1] Many of us have experienced "cabin fever" and various mental health problems because of serial lockdowns and confinement. Some of us may have been sick, had close encounters with death or had someone close to us die. The pandemic has forced patience on us and made us realize

---

[1] Manfred F. R. Kets de Vries (2020). *Journeys into Coronavirus Land: Lessons from a Pandemic*. eBook: https://www.kdvi.com/research_items/859.

that patience is one of the more difficult challenges of being human. The current global crisis has made patience the subject of a great social experiment—because our twenty-first-century world is not a patient one. On the contrary, we live in a world of instant gratification. We are no longer prepared to wait for our food, our goods, or our entertainment. Many of us don't give ourselves the time to read a novel or follow an unfolding television drama. Instead, we prefer to read mini articles, look at YouTube clips or binge watch whole series in one sitting. When our needs aren't met immediately, we rapidly become frustrated.

Patience—the ability to remain calm in the face of disappointment, adversity, or distress—has lost a lot of its value with the disappearance of the conditions that demand it. So why bother with it? Well, as the events of the last eighteen months alone should show, patience has many benefits. Patience allows us to process difficult situations better. It helps us get our thoughts in order and our feelings under control. It helps us avoid angry outbursts and snap judgments, resulting in better decisions. When we are patient, we are seen as more relaxed and friendly. We have better relationships at work and with our friends and family.

Social psychologists have recognized that patience comes in various guises. They differentiate three kinds of patience.[2] The first is "interpersonal patience," or the ability to treat annoying people with equanimity. The second is "life hardship patience," or the patience to overcome serious, long-term setbacks in life (like the results of medical treatment or expectations of job promotion). The third is "daily hassles patience," or how we deal with "trivial" life events, like getting stuck in traffic or facing long lines at the supermarket.

In a nutshell, patience enables us to manage stress and is good for our mental health, which is why it is part of Homo sapiens' standard emotional repertoire. Taking an evolutionary development perspective, good things happened to people who could wait.

Impatience, on the other hand, is unhelpful in most scenarios although perhaps it is inevitable in our day-and-age. Our world has become so much more complicated than it used to be. Our social lives and personal schedules have become more complex. This increasing complexity means it is much more likely that the different parts of our lives will collide. Given the pressures we live with, we are less likely to wait for good things to happen. But we need to remember that impatience raises our cortisol levels, triggering our flight or fight response, which creates feelings of anxiety, anger, rage, and even panic.

---

[2] Sarah Schnitker (2012). An examination of patience and well-being, *The Journal of Positive Psychology*, 7 (4), 263–280.

It can damage our reputation, relationships, and decision-making, and escalate already difficult situations. In fact, impatience may well be the cause of many of the difficulties and unhappiness in the world today.

Not everyone is impatient to the same degree. Some people are consistently more impatient than others and get visibly more agitated when faced with life's challenges. Such behavior seems to be part of their personality makeup. However, context is everything. It might well be that in some chaotic environments, where long-term planning doesn't pay off, impatient people might do better than patient people, while in more stable environments, patient people might do better than those who are impatient.

Flexing the Patience "Muscle"

Fortunately, patience isn't something you are born with. It is something that can be learned, although it will take time and effort. Some of you, without realizing it, have already had the opportunity to flex your patience muscle by having children.

Although the wait for a vaccine against the coronavirus may have been the litmus test of your patience, generally speaking, teaching yourself to become more patient will be beneficial in any situation, at work or at home. The road to acquiring more patience, however, can be a long one, and those who want to see results immediately may not be willing to walk it. But it will be well worth the effort. Practicing patience will make you more effective in dealing with adversity, and the many frustrations that come with living.

Discover Your Patience Triggers

You may have clear triggers that make you impatient. These could be specific people, situations, or even certain words. The physical indicators suggesting that something has set you off include fast breathing, muscle tension, and hand clenching. A sudden mood change can be another indicator. For example, you may suddenly become irritable, angry, or anxious. Whatever your triggers are, they can rush you into things, and encourage you to make snap decisions, clear signs that your impatience is gaining the upper hand. But while you are going into impatience overdrive, try to remember that yelling, swearing, threatening, or belittling will not get you where you want to be. Once you recognize your impatience triggers, you can apply some of the practices listed here.

Reframe the Situation

Feeling impatient is not just an automatic emotional response; it also involves conscious thought processes, so you can try consciously to regulate your emotions by reframing challenging situations. Try to focus on the bigger picture. Ask yourself whether the cause of your impatience will matter in the longer term? Will it even matter a few hours from now? If you can remind yourself that whatever is irritating you or happening right now is not the end of the world and doesn't interfere with the bigger picture, you might be able to control your impatience.

Fantasize

Many situations that demand patience simply require you to wait, such as standing at security lines at the airport, or queuing to get into a restaurant. In these scenarios, there's often nothing you can do to speed things up. You could fill that time productively by distracting yourself, using daydreams or other forms of visualization. For example, when you are frustrated by this "daily hassle impatience," imagine places or situations that make you happy or calm you down. Or you could go through an imagining exercise: try visualizing that you are in a stressful situation where you're likely to lose your patience. Now imagine how your most confident, calm, collected self would handle such a situation then act that out.

Practice Empathy

In many cases, your impatience will be triggered by something interpersonal. If so, a little empathy can go a long way. Remind yourself of the advantages of being empathic rather than impatient. Being empathic requires giving up a self-centered view of the world; it implies that you need to focus and pay attention to the feelings of the other person. If you can act like this, you will connect with the other person's emotions. In an empathic state, we produce a near-magical neurotransmitter—oxytocin—which promotes feelings of affection, social bonding and well-being, all key to successfully negotiating and resolving conflict. Learning to communicate with empathy will take you a long way toward building more positivity in your relationships and reducing your stress levels.

Practice Gratitude

Gratitude is one of the most important and effective motivating factors in everyone's life. Somewhere, sometime, whether through their actions or comments, someone has done good things for you. When you are in a situation that triggers your impatience, shift your focus, and think consciously about the things that are going well in your life. Think about the people who have helped make it this way. Saying "thank you" will make them—and you—feel good. Showing gratitude will help your well-being in several ways, such as helping you to build new relationships or boost current ones, to forgive yourself and others, and to reduce your anger. Expressing gratitude is key to your personal and professional mental health and an excellent antidote to impatience. What's more, when you express gratitude, you become better at delaying gratification—another way to flex your patience muscle. It will help you neutralize your aggressive urges and boost your prosocial behavior.

Use Humor

Joy is an important emotion to include in your repertoire and you can create joy through humor, an emotion that, given the choice, you should try to select over anger, fear, resentment, envy, or sadness. When you find yourself in a difficult situation or in disagreement with someone who makes you increasingly impatient, it will be a great help to find the humor in what's going on. Humor can become the neutralizer that defuses fraught occasions. It changes your perspective. It allows you to step back and see things more clearly. Things become lighter when you can laugh about them and take them less seriously. Laughing is like taking a deep breath and bringing things down to earth. It is a very effective way to calm stressful situations.

Be Realistic

You may have found yourself in situations where you were genuinely stuck; where there was little you could do to change whatever was happening to you. Stuff happens, and life isn't always fair. If you find yourself in such a situation, you might remind yourself of the famous Serenity Prayer: "God, grant me serenity to accept the things I cannot change, courage to change the things I can, and wisdom to know the difference." Frankly, accepting situations over which you have no control may be one of the most difficult tests of your patience. But you can continue to push forward while accepting that there are things beyond your control. You can adapt and adjust to your present circumstances.

Practice Mindfulness

Whenever you bring awareness to what you're directly experiencing via your senses, or to your state of mind via your thoughts and emotions, you're being mindful. Mindfulness refers to your ability to be fully present, to be aware of where you are and what you're doing. It helps you not to be overly reactive or overwhelmed by what's going on around you. In other words, mindfulness is a useful and readily available tool for dealing with practically any negative emotion, including impatience.

Ask Others for Help

Finally, if you find your feelings of impatience insurmountable, you can always ask others for their help. You might feel fine about involving your friends and family members but if not, or if they are not equipped to do so, you may prefer to turn to a coach or psychotherapist for assistance. These professionals will help you discover your trigger points and guide you toward controlling your impatience.

Practicing patience may start as a means of concealing your impatience. But practicing patience in everyday situations will not only make life more pleasant in the here and now; it will also pave the way toward a more pleasant future when patience comes more naturally. The global pandemic has tested everyone's patience but it also showed us that we are capable of withstanding an unseen enemy that completely disrupts our social norms and fabric. If we continue to flex our patience muscle until everybody has received the vaccine, we will make post-Covid life more livable for all of us.

6

Groundhog Day: A Learning Experience

> *The patient cannot remember the whole of what is repressed in him, and what he cannot remember may be precisely the essential part of it… He is obliged to repeat the repressed material as a contemporary experience instead of remembering it as something in the past.*
> —Sigmund Freud

As a psychoanalyst, psychotherapist, executive coach, and consultant, I work to help my clients cope more effectively with problems that interfere with their emotional and physical health. I want them to make the changes that are needed to improve their quality of life. These are typically everyday challenges, such as mapping out their career, being more effective as a leader, dealing better with negative behavior patterns, strengthening their stress management skills, and even improving their parenting capabilities and navigating important relationships. Of course, the objectives of these encounters depend on each person's unique situation. Every intervention plan is different.

My type of work has been more in demand and proved more relevant than ever during the pandemic. Lockdown and the disruption of normality have created a generalized sense of Groundhog Day, a real event that has become associated with the apparently endless recurrence of unfortunate events. At the same time, Groundhog Days can be learning experiences, bringing opportunities for self-reflection and conscious resetting of our lives.

Few of us can be unfamiliar with the term Groundhog Day. It is the title of a cult movie in which the main character, a disaffected weather forecaster called Phil Connors, played by Bill Murray, is sent to Punxsutawney in

Pennsylvania to report on the annual Groundhog Day, when the emergence (or not) of a groundhog from its lair is said to predict an early or late spring. Connors wrongly predicts fine weather only to be stuck in the town following a blizzard. Worse, he finds himself stuck in a time loop. He relives the same day (Groundhog Day) over and over again, making the same mistakes. With each iteration of the day, he undergoes a realization that the control he thought he had over his life was just an illusion.

The plot of the movie is how Connors will get out of town. First, he makes a conscious decision to take greater control over his life, which leads him to experiment with small but new ways of dealing with the recurring events of the day. He discovers that if he makes slight changes to his behavior, people will respond to him differently, opening all kinds of possibilities for moving forward. The moral of the movie is that we need to wake up and be more open to exploring beyond the safety of our established routines to learn new things and reinvent ourselves.

In more than one way, *Groundhog Day* can also be seen as a metaphor for what happens during the coaching and therapeutic process. A question I always ask my clients is: Do you want to remain stuck in routines or do you want to use this space to look beyond for redemptive, reparative possibilities in your life?

During coaching and therapeutic conversations, we tell and revisit our stories and become aware that we are reliving the same patterns in our life. Awareness of the routine scripts we tell ourselves, allows us to break free and try a different narrative—one that will make us feel more alive and to try different things.

Similarly, the reflective moments that have been created by the pandemic could help us to transcend the repetitive thoughts and behaviors that keep us stuck in a rut. Whereas most of us may go semi-automatically through most of our (very similar) days, Phil Connors is stuck in the same day, and has the luxury to experiment with new ways of behaving until he gets it right. At the end of the film, he has an emotional breakthrough, discovering his more authentic self, in which creativity, intimacy, empathy and compassion are part of the package.

Groundhog Day, as well as being very funny, is a personal development success story. It shows the transformation of its main character from being completely self-absorbed and cynical about life into someone attuned to the environment and those around him. It shows that when we see all the good things life has to offer with fresh eyes, we can move beyond skepticism and resentment. As Phil moves from an inward state of selfishness toward his ability to look outwards and give to those around him, he gets out of his psychic loop to feel more authentic and alive.

Life during the pandemic has presented us with many challenges, some of which have led to despondency, helplessness, and hopelessness. We may have been overwhelmed by our fears; we may even have had a sense that life is meaningless. The stress confinement and the disruption of our daily life have caused may even have triggered addictive behavior and harmful relationships, all of which induce depressive reactions.

But it doesn't have to be this way. We always have choices in life, even when we are being undermined by a sub-microscopic enemy. We aren't just victims of fate. We have the power to change what matters in our lives. Wasting our time on anger, regrets, worries, and grudges is counterproductive. Instead, it is more helpful to appreciate the things we do have. Such an outlook will encourage us to experiment with life. And regardless of whether the changes we implement are big or small, as long as we maintain an open mind and continually invest time in our personal growth and development, we will continue to improve our lives until the day we die.

In the movie, there is a turning point, when something small shifts in Phil Connors' mind and he stops following his now daily, repetitive, script to trying something new. Thus, if you want to escape your own Groundhog Day, you need to create similar tipping points. Meaningful talks with good friends and family members can be a highly effective strategy to get out of a rut. Exploring and unpacking your story can have a cathartic, healing effect. Also, you can lean on the experiences of people who have come before you, past and present, who have overcome difficult challenges. Through their examples, you may come to realize that change is possible. Then there is professional help. There are many helping professionals available (psychotherapists and coaches) who can provide support. Furthermore, there is always the altruistic route. Paradoxically, helping others is a very effective way of helping yourself. As *Groundhog Day* illustrates, self-gratification alone won't make you feel better about yourself; you need to work with a worthy purpose. Indeed, a 2021 report from the UN Department of Global Communications noted that "[a] wave of solidarity … spread across Europe" in response to the pandemic, citing the example of France in particular, where the number of volunteers on one platform doubled in 2020, and recording "hundreds of thousands of new volunteers across the world, including 48,000 new sign-ups in the Netherlands and 60,000 in Italy."[1]

---

[1] https://www.un.org/en/coronavirus/covid-19-drives-global-surge-volunteering.

As *Groundhog Day* and these statistics demonstrate, it is advisable to become an active participant in whatever life presents you with. They show the real importance of seizing the day, learning to enjoy every minute of your life, to breathe, think, enjoy, and love. Don't wait for something beyond yourself to make you happy. It is all up to you. Just think how different your life would be if you stopped worrying about things you can't control and started focusing on the things you can. When you pause and look around you, you will see that you are continually presented with opportunities to grow, to find purpose and meaning, and to experience happiness. It is up to you to free yourself from the prison of bad habits, dare to be the best you can be, and act.

7

The Labyrinth of Forgetfulness

> ...[We] reached the country of the Lotus-eaters, a race that eat the flowery Lotus fruit...Now these natives had no intention of killing my comrades; what they did was to give them some Lotus to taste. Those who ate the honeyed fruit of the plant lost any wish to come back and bring us news. All they now wanted was to stay where they were with the Lotus-eaters, to browse on the Lotus, and to forget all thoughts of return...
> —Homer

> Those who make the worst use of their time are the first to complain of its brevity.
> —Jean de La Bruyère

Odysseus, the hero of Homer's epic poem *The Odyssey*, tells how adverse north winds blew his ship off course, and he and his men ended up in the land of the lotus-eaters. The inhabitants ate lotus flowers, which put them in a state of drug-induced forgetfulness. Members of Odysseus' crew who ate the flowers became similarly oblivious. They forgot their home and family and declared that they were happy to stay with the lotus-eaters. But Odysseus, seeing what was happening, dragged his men forcibly back to the ship, chained them to the oars, and immediately set out to sea. He realized that if he hadn't taken his men, they would never have returned home. They would have forgotten all their memories and be forever stuck in a state of unmindfulness.

Did lockdown have a similar effect on your state of mind? How did quarantine and isolation feel to you? Did it affect your sense of time? Did you become forgetful? Can you remember your first day in isolation? Does it feel like a lifetime ago? Or does it feel like yesterday?

During the pandemic, many people who were forced to stay home noticed something strange had happened to the passing of time. Some complained that days seemed to drag on for ever although the weeks seemed to fly past. Some people felt bored, and had nothing to do, while others were busier than ever—the obvious examples those working in hospitals on the front line of the pandemic or parents having to combine a full work schedule with home-schooling their children.

When we remember past times, a distinction can be made between two processes: the experience of an event and the recollection of it. Depending on the memorability of the experience, the same event can appear to be passing quickly or slowly. Given these very different perceptions, the pandemic has been a very interesting time laboratory.

If you're one of those people forced to stay at home during the pandemic, your perception of time will have a lot to do with the way your world shrank down to essentials—staying put for most of your day and going out only for exercise or grocery shopping. Obviously, you no longer took part in more invigorating activities, such as putting the world to rights in a café, meeting new people at a bar, having dinner with friends, going to a concert, seeing an exhibition, or embarking on a journey. When you do the same thing day after day—the new normal for many in quarantine or lockdown—there's no need to remember the specifics of each day. Even if time seems to pass slowly, nothing is likely to stand out when you look back, causing you to perceive that time has in fact passed by too quickly.

So, what factors affect our experience of time? What makes time go faster, or slower?

The Neural Circuit

Our consciousness of time develops during childhood, a period when we form our capacity for attention and short-term memory in the hippocampus and prefrontal cortex of the brain. In childhood, due to the overload of new stimuli we receive, we dedicate significantly more brain power to configuring mental inputs from the outside world. Because our developing brains take more time to process all this new information, time seems to last longer. But as we get older, and there are fewer new stimuli to integrate, we perceive time as passing more rapidly. This explains why we might clearly remember those endless summer days of childhood, while we can forget what happened only yesterday. Our brains have processed these experiences quite differently.

An additional factor that influences our perception of time is that the brain cells that produce dopamine—the regions that determine the workings of our internal clock—begin to deteriorate as we age and the pathways that transmit information become less effective. Also, our vision and memory are no longer what they once were. As a result, as we get older, these changes in the way we process information—plus the lack of new mental images—contribute to the feeling that time is speeding up.

The Role of Novelty

Novelty plays an essential role in our perception of time. It also contributes to the creation of new memories. While an impactful or novel event will be experienced as passing far too quickly but remembered as lasting longer, the opposite is the case with less novelty. For example, humdrum, uneventful days are experienced as passing slowly, but when recalled seem to have just flown by. In other words, without novelty within a given time period, we will recall fewer memories, making for a very different time experience.

Childhood is a period in time of many "first" experiences: our "first" ice cream, our "first" visit to the zoo, our "first" plane ride, for example. These memories stick, making time seem to last much longer. In contrast, the fewer novel events we experience, the more time flies. Another Christmas already. Where did the last year go? Look at the children! They are grown up! How did that happen?

The idea that novelty influences our perception of time is reflected in sayings like "time flies when you're having fun" but "a watched pot never boils." In other words, the less attention we pay to the time dimension, the slower our internal clock runs relative to the passage of physical time. In fact, the greater the emotional impact a memory has, the longer our perception of its duration will be. This explains why a weekend spent at home has a different perceptual memory from a weekend spent at an exciting vacation resort.

The significant emotional impact of novelty suggests that we can manipulate our perception of the speed at which time passes. Our evaluation of time will differ depending on our emotional state at the time of evaluation. Depending on whether we're bored or elated, time will slow down or expand. Most of us know that time appears to pass slowly while we are doing something tedious but passes all too quickly when we are engaged in something we're passionate about. Furthermore, the way we perceive time is also affected by the way we anticipate future events. If we're looking forward to something exciting, the time we must wait for the event to occur can seem to pass unbearably slowly. But when we know we're going to have to deal with something disagreeable, the event seems to come much sooner than we want.

Cognitive Illusions

It's clear that our perception of the passage of time is a cognitive illusion. The greater the novelty of the perceptual information we receive, the greater its emotional impact and the more attention we pay to it. This explains the illusion why many of our "first" experiences seemed to have been endless. Faced with new situations our brain will record more richly detailed memories, so that in recollection the event appears slower than it actually was. The more novel stimuli we encounter, the longer it takes for our brains to process the information. In other words, the higher the demand required of a cognitive task, the corresponding period of time seems (at least in retrospect) to last longer. Thus, our changed perception of time comes down to the fact that adulthood doesn't feature the constant, never-ending discovery of new things that's inherent to childhood.

Furthermore, the perception that time speeds up as we age may also be the effect of a "logarithmic scale" relating time to age. For example, a year to a 10-year-old feels much longer than a year to a 50-year-old because the older we get, the smaller one year is as a percentage of our total life. In fact, we are constantly comparing time intervals to the total amount of time we've lived. However, this scale does not negate the effects of novelty, attention, and their emotional impact. There may be truth in the argument that it doesn't matter how long our life is, what's important is what we fill it with.

Managing Our Time

Knowing what we do about the passing of time has important implications for the way we lead our lives. This is particularly true now, since the pandemic has created the illusion that time is passing too quickly. It isn't really, of course, but the illusion is caused by the lack of novelty and action, which prevents our creating memorable events. Lockdowns and quarantine limit our options and possibilities for experience. But this doesn't mean that we should abandon the pursuit of novelty. There are still many interesting things we can do. If we create new "firsts" to keep our brain active, we can alter our perception of time.

As a starter, an obvious challenge is to learn to be at ease with being with ourselves—to spend time exploring our inner world—to go inward bound.

Dealing with solitude can be a great learning experience. Having more time for ourselves gives us an opportunity to figure out what we're all about. We sometimes forget how unlonely being alone can be. It can be nice, however, to enjoy our own presence. Time out for self-reflection gives us an opportunity to tune in to ourselves, to find out what's truly important to us.

If we are feeling anxious and have difficulty with being by ourselves, it can be helpful to find new purpose. Purpose provides focus and can bring new structure to our lives. We can use the time at our disposal to try out new things. For example, if we've always wanted to have a go at pottery, writing or any other quarantine-friendly activity, now is the time to try it. We can plan events to look forward to after quarantine is over. And we can always create virtual social events like a virtual happy hour, virtual pub quiz or virtual discussion group—something to look forward to all week.

There is also a lot to be said for eco-therapy. Long walks in nature can be very therapeutic—and memorable. We are all part of the web of life; we are all connected to and impacted by the natural environment. Exposure to nature is important to our mental health. Spending time outdoors improves low moods and promotes relaxation and calm. The same observation can be made about meditation, becoming more intensely aware of what we're sensing and what we're feeling in the moment.

Overall, the pandemic has been a rare opportunity to reset our inner clock. Knowing that the passage of time is a cognitive illusion could have helped us to make the best of it. As human beings, we will always experience the push and pull of *neophilia*, the attraction of new things, and *neophobia*, the fear of new things. It is important to keep on reminding ourselves that novelty can be a great way of intensifying memory—making it feel that our life lasts longer. The less frequently we do something, the deeper the memory will burrow in.

Unfortunately, too few people want novelty—they want the reassurance of familiarity instead. They resist change. They would do better to remind themselves that newness is important. The pandemic, notwithstanding its very tragic nature, also offers all of us a great opportunity to try out new things. It enables us to make a creative change in our lifestyle, to do things that we may never have thought of doing before or have been too hesitant to try. And we should start today.

8

The Triumph of Hope over Experience

> *Love looks not with the eyes, but with the mind. And therefore is winged Cupid painted blind.*
> —William Shakespeare

> *There is always some madness in love. But there is also always some reason in madness.*
> —Friedrich Nietzsche

> *Marriage is the triumph of imagination over intelligence. Second marriage is the triumph of hope over experience.*
> —Oscar Wilde, after Samuel Johnson

While ostensibly discussing business issues, many of the executives I deal with go off the rails—if that's the right term to use. At some point, they begin talking about problems much closer to home, basically, their relationship with their partner. Whenever someone in one of my seminars starts to talk about relationship problems, the other participants are quick to jump in with advice and more than happy to share lessons they've learned from their own relationships. My conclusion, after participating in so many of these discussions, is that Prince or Princess Charming is as rare as hen's teeth and that the ideal partner is an illusion. These discussions are fueled by the fact that the mismatch between ideal and actual partners can be very costly and stressful for both individuals and wider society. So why do so many people choose the wrong partner? And why do people hang on to relationships that make them unhappy?

Let me summarize what I have learned from these discussions. But before I start, a reminder: the famous injunction "Know thyself" is highly relevant to partner relationships. Only by knowing yourself will you recognize your shortcomings, strengths, and weaknesses, and understand what motivates you and what doesn't. Knowing what you're all about will be important if you are thinking of making a commitment—whether to a person or to something else.

Lesson 1: Making the Right Choice

A large part of the selection process is physical attractiveness, which drives sexual desire. However, getting into a relationship based on great sex, although sex is important, isn't a good enough basis for a long-term commitment. In fact, the *coup de foudre*—love at first sight—could even be viewed as a temporary psychotic state. If it happens to you, you should remind yourself that lust can be extremely misleading. You are at the mercy of sex hormones, which have the same effect as steroids, making your sex drive work overtime and rational decision-making go out the window. It might help to think of unstoppable love affairs as nature's way of tricking us into doing insane and irrational things in order to procreate.

A solid dose of reality will put the brakes on this emotional helter-skelter. After all, you're not going to be in sexual overdrive every day for the rest of your life. Sexual desire fluctuates. A particularly solid dose of reality to your sexual acrobatics is to realize that you could end up with children. Before you fall head over heels in love, or give way to your sexual urge, try asking yourself whether you want to have kids with this specific sexual partner. And while you're doing that, ask yourself whether you would consider staying with this partner for the rest of your life. Both those questions risk having the effect of a cold shower but will be a reality check at the very least. Love at first sight might be a shortcut to fulfilling the biological imperative to procreate before a couple has enough time to confront each party's faults. If you can pause for thought, you might realize that a long-term relationship needs much more than sexual passion.

Steady, long-term commitment to someone else, whatever challenges life throws at you, needs intimacy and care of a very different order than passion and desire. It means accepting the good, the bad and the ugly of your partner and your shared experience. The danger of a relationship based solely on sexual desire is that it may be over the instant both parties are no longer crazy about each other. You or your partner might start looking for a way out. For some people, sexual passion depends on novelty.

Lesson 2: Why Marry?

Getting married because everyone else you know seems to be getting married is no reason to leap into a commitment yourself. It's true that staying single when everyone else is coupling up can be a challenge. You may come under considerable social pressure to do the same. Many will recall the nightmare dinner party in *Bridget Jones's Diary*[1] when, surrounded by "smug marrieds," the heroic singleton is told she should "hurry up and get sprogged up you know, old girl," because "time's running out." If you are still firmly single while others are pairing up, you may find your friends and family start to feel uncomfortable around you. For many reasons, they'd like you to be part of a couple. Perhaps unconsciously, or not so unconsciously, they might envy your freedom. You might remind them of more carefree periods in their lives. This may explain why they suddenly find an interest in matchmaking for you. Getting hitched due to group pressure isn't the answer but at the same time group pressure can make you feel miserable and prey to the fear that if you don't find a partner, others might think you're a loser. Resisting this sort of pressure isn't easy. But resist it you must, because a relationship needs much more solid ground than simply doing what everybody else is doing.

Lesson 3: Fear of Ending up Alone

This sort of pressure from others might well make you afraid you will end up alone. You might feel compelled to lock a partner down fast or be tempted to fall for the first person who pays you some attention. But although hitching up with someone might help you feel better, and take that pressure off, unless there are other good reasons for being together, it could be a prescription for real misery. You could end up no longer alone but truly lonely, with someone who is emotionally unavailable.

Even though "loneliness" and "being alone" sound alike, they are two very different concepts. Loneliness is a psychological condition, while being alone is a physical state—you can be alone but not lonely and you can feel lonely even when surrounded by people. Being alone means solitude—not loneliness—the experience of enjoying your own company. It might even indicate a state of peace, especially if you have a rich inner life. Loneliness is very different. It suggests estrangement from others—the inability to relate to other human beings. Before making a commitment, ask yourself whether this

---

[1] Helen Fielding (2014), *Bridget Jones's Diary*. London: Picador.

person makes you feel less lonely. And never make a choice out of fear—the fear of ending up alone.

Lesson 4: Unfinished Business

If you feel you are pushed toward commitment, take the time to consider whether you might be responding to some unfinished psychological business and, if so, to what and to what degree. A warning bell should ring if you feel it has to do with a sense of feeling incomplete. Do not delude yourself that having a partner will complete you. Hoping to find the missing part of your personal jigsaw in someone else is a bad idea and can lead to very messy, even toxic, situations.

For example, a highly neurotic choice would be to enter a relationship based on the (not necessarily conscious) wish to put some unfinished business right. You might have an unconscious need to repair an untenable situation you experienced while you were growing up. Ironically, although you may be determined not to repeat the mistakes your parents made, you may unconsciously do exactly that. What's more, you might be attracted to a partner who has both your caregivers' positive and negative traits in order to resolve your unmet childhood needs. This need for reparation, or fixing, explains why someone raised by a mother with an alcohol disorder might be drawn toward a partner exhibiting similar traits, compelled by the unconscious desire to "fix" her, as he would have liked to have "fixed" his mother. This type of unconscious recognition is not unusual. As one executive told me, "I knew as soon as I met Rita that, like me, she had been brought up by a parent with an alcohol disorder, before we ever spoke about it." However, there is little hope for a relationship if you see your partner as some kind of change project.

Of course, initial attraction may be based on complementarities in character, in that opposites attract, suggesting the possibility of widening experiences. All relationships can have a compensatory element to them, but these psychological dynamics, which could contain the seeds of a neurotic entanglement, should be limited. The impulse to use a relationship to soothe your own emotional distress, to engage in self-sacrifice, to focus on another's needs, to suppress your own emotions, or to try to control or fix another person's problems, will inevitably lead to co-dependency. Such a relationship might seem superficially harmonious, but if each party ends up being the other's emotional hostage, it will lead to bitterness and resentment. A relationship based on constant and mutual sacrifice will damage both parties and is likely to be unstable and short term.

Having said all that, there are situations when toxic co-dependent relationships appear to have an inherent stability. In such instances, both parties are locked in an implicit arrangement whereby they tolerate each other's dysfunctional behavior. But forming and staying in such a relationship is not a sign of maturity and it doesn't help you to become a person in your own right. So, before you make any serious commitment to someone else, try to figure out the extent to which your choice is guided by your past demons. Ask yourself what role you hope your partner will play in taming those demons. Furthermore, if one of those demons involves the impulse to save or change your partner, you should be honest with yourself about this. Needing to change your partner is inherently disrespectful, to both your partner and you. Stable, mature relationships require two emotionally well-adjusted individuals who recognize that each is a person in his or her own right. That means two people with their own identity, their own interests, and their own perspectives, doing things by and for themselves, on their own time.

Lesson 5: Mutual Respect

Strong relationships are built on mutual respect. In fact, if there isn't mutual respect, each party will start doubting the other and even hiding things from them for fear of criticism, so that secrets become par for the course. Once this dynamic sets in, it could mark the beginning of a failed relationship. To cushion the ups and downs that are part of any relationship, it's imperative that each party truly respects the other and each holds the other in high esteem. You should believe in one another—often more than you might believe in yourselves. In other words, respect for your partner and respect for yourself are intertwined. After all, if you don't respect yourself, you might not feel worthy of the respect of your partner. Mutual respect also implies that you appreciate your partner's work ethic, creativity, intelligence, and core values. Mutual respect is the safe foundation on which you can build trust, resilience, and long-term commitment—important when times get tough.

Lesson 6: Trust

Most people mention trust in the context of jealousy and fidelity. Of course, if trust is broken for these reasons, it takes quite some time to rebuild it. And if you break trust enough times and fail to own up and set about correcting your mistakes, it is doubtful you will ever get it fully back again, whatever you do.

However, trust goes much deeper than questions of fidelity. It is critical to any relationship. Consider other situations: would your partner have the grit and loyalty to hang in there when the going gets tough? Could you trust them to take care of you when you get sick? Would you trust them to take care of your children, your money, and your possessions? Can you trust them not to exploit your vulnerability? If you can acknowledge each other's vulnerabilities, and have a good understanding of each other's insecurities, you will have a solid trust-based relationship through which you can help each other cope.

Lesson 7: Forgiveness

Each and every one of us is a flawed human being. Inevitably, you are going to make mistakes. Therefore, if you want to enjoy a lasting relationship with someone you value—a person you want to spend your life with—you need to develop your ability to forgive. Forgiveness is a key component in any healthy relationship. It means letting go of the desire, the need, or the "right" to want punishment or restitution for a perceived offense. Building a case against your partner, listing every mistake he or she has made, would be a grave error: once you allow little seeds of anger to be planted, they will grow into a level of resentment that will eventually break your relationship. However, if you can forgive, rather than holding a grudge or harboring resentment, you will be able to restore what has been lost.

Couples who practice forgiveness will have a much deeper relationship. They won't get stuck in a vicious, destructive cycle of blame and resentment. Forgiveness provides a unique opportunity to deepen your relationship and strengthen what you have together. Forgiveness allows you to move beyond your hurt and guilt, to heal, and to grow.

Lesson 8: Communication

When people talk about the need for "good communication," they often mean being willing to have uncomfortable conversations, being able to say out loud that something in your relationship, including sexuality, bothers you. If you're able to have these kinds of conversations, you build trust, and trust builds intimacy. When things aren't working well in your relationship, it isn't enough to talk about it with other people; that may help you get some clarity, but it's most important to talk to each other.

There will be arguments in every relationship. The question is not how you can avoid them but how you will deal with them when they happen. The goal is constructive communication: no name-calling, no personal criticism, no blame, no contempt and no dragging up earlier fights. Resist the urge to be "right" or to think in terms of "winning." Whatever the problem may be, making your partner feel like a loser won't solve anything.

Obviously, the preferred option is to prevent arguments arising, but if you decide to fight, pick your battles wisely. Ask yourself, is what you're upset about a little thing or a big thing? Is it worth fighting for? If you persist in arguing about little things, you could find yourself arguing endlessly. So, if you get caught up in an argument, try to be constructively engaged and stay positive. Over time, you might find you develop rules of engagement that prevent future arguments.

Lesson 9: Space

Individual space is essential in a relationship. However, some people are afraid to give their partner freedom and independence. Often, this derives from insecurity, neediness, or a lack of trust. Their reasoning is that if their partner has too much space, they may not want to be with them anymore. The more uncomfortable you are with your own self-worth—being anxious of deserving to be in the relationship—the more you will try to control your partner's behavior. Should you feel this need, you should remind yourself that imprisonment never works. Too much confinement will only increase the other party's desire for freedom. Unless each of you has a life of your own, it will be hard to have a life together. Each of you should have your own interests, friends, support network, and hobbies; but a degree of overlap is also very important. A successful relationship needs common interests but having different interests means you will always have something to talk about.

Lesson 10: Growing Together

What you appreciate in your twenties may be quite different when you are in your thirties, forties, fifties, or sixties. The truth is, when you commit yourself to someone, you don't really know exactly who they are. You may know them to a certain degree today, but you can't have any idea who they will be in five or ten years or more. As time passes, each of you will evolve and grow in different and unexpected ways. But whatever those changes turn out to be, always welcome your partner's growth and development. As for your own, you should be ready to go to great lengths not to get stuck. Work on yourself and make sure you are bringing your partner with you. In a successful relationship, both parties will embrace and respect the changes that come with growing older, and above all talk about them.

* * *

All ten of these lessons share a common message—tolerance for imperfection. In other words, there's no point looking for the fictive Mr. or Ms. Perfect; you should be looking for Mr. or Ms. Good Enough. All relationships are imperfect, messy affairs for the simple reason that they involve imperfect, messy people who want different things at different times, in different ways. In that respect, relationships are a roller-coaster ride of constant ups and downs. However, if you can stay together long enough, the downs will become less dramatic, and the ups more pleasurable.

While you are looking out for Mr. or Ms. Good Enough, keep in mind the qualities you look for in a good friendship, including their and your own capacity for commitment and change. Relationships last if neither party is too set in their ways. The ability to negotiate and accommodate each other's narcissistic needs cannot be emphasized enough. The couple system should be seen as an emotional container, within which you and your partner engage in mutual mirroring, holding and dialogue. If you can do this, it will be easier to face together life's existential realities. Furthermore, a capacity for humor and playfulness will also help buffer the frustrations of daily life. The relationships that enjoy these qualities are the ones that last longest.

Some kind of division of labor, where both parties share responsibilities, is essential in relationships that work. Both of you should figure out what you're good at and what you love, or hate doing and make arrangements accordingly. Similarly, you should take care to regulate the intensity of the relationship: balance time together with time for yourself; do meaningful activities together but make time for your own interests.

Finally, a reminder that the biological imperative that drives pairing up is procreation. You will likely have kids, at which point a bomb will go off in even the best and strongest of relationships. The greatest danger with creating these hostages to fortune is that you will make them the only focus of your life and your partner, despite having played an equal part in lighting the fuse, will be sidelined. If you aren't careful, this could cost you your relationship. You need to avoid falling into that trap. Continue to pay attention to your partner. Make time for each other. The best way to raise healthy and happy kids is to maintain a healthy and happy partnership. Good kids don't make a good partnership, but a good partnership makes good kids. Always make your relationship with your partner a top priority.

Part II

Leadership

9

How Is Your Shadow Side Treating You?

How can I be substantial if I do not cast a shadow? I must have a dark side also if I am to be whole. Where love rules, there is no will to power, and where power predominates, love is lacking. The one is the shadow of the other.
—Carl Jung

In the social jungle of human existence, there is no feeling of being alive without a sense of identity.
—Erik Erikson

To many, John seemed to have high ethical values and to be a true role model. He was a star student: disciplined, hardworking, and very achievement oriented. He was also active outside his schoolwork, his boy scout activities a prime example. As time went by, he graduated from the Ivy League college of his choice and joined an investment bank. When accepting this position, he claimed that he wanted to go beyond being merely a financial engineer—to prove that investment bankers could also be highly ethical. He had always believed that the financial shenanigans that had negatively affected the image of the profession had been the work of a few bad apples. To prove his point, John decided to become actively involved in several NGOs, activities that added to his stellar reputation.

Suddenly, however, John appeared to undergo a strange metamorphosis. Some people thought his marriage to Anne explained a dramatic change in his outlook (she was perceived as demanding and materialistic). Others even wondered whether substance abuse might account for the remarkable turnaround in John's mindset and behavior. But whatever the reasons for his change in outlook, soon after their wedding, John quit the bank to join the office of a notorious businessman, someone whom he had previously labeled "a business highwayman" who took advantage of other people's vulnerabilities. In many ways, this tycoon was the opposite of everything John had supposedly stood for. But in a recent Bloomberg interview, to the great disappointment of his friends, John had distorted known facts and vehemently defended his new boss' behavior and even his shady activities.

Unfortunately, John is not an outlier. Similar transformations seem to occur regularly, not only in the business world but also in the world of politics, where people often trade principle for position: a telling example is the transformation in the understanding of basic US values among large numbers of Republican politicians. Many people like to be close to sources of power and are willing to pay the moral fee for being at the epicenter of the action. This raises the question whether doing good and doing right was ever high on their personal agenda. Perhaps their ethical orientation was always superficial. Unfortunately, we see how frequently and completely the lure of power, glory and money overwhelms any call to conscience.

So, what are the psychological dynamics behind these transformations? Why do these people undergo apparently spontaneous changes in character?

For a long time, John presented himself as a champion of goodness, but his turnaround suggests that something very different was happening to him on the inside. Could it be that overall, people are less good than they imagine themselves to be? Under the social mask they wear, is there a hidden, darker, side that surfaces in the right conditions?

In extreme cases, the term "dissociative identity disorder" is used to describe what happens to people when their darker side comes to the fore. Dissociative identity disorder is characterized by presenting at least two distinct and relatively enduring personalities. It involves a severe form of mental dissociation that contributes to a lack of connection between a person's thoughts, memories, feelings, actions, or sense of identity. Early childhood trauma, involving various kinds of abuse, often seems to be the root cause of such disorders.

The psychoanalyst Carl Jung popularized the term "the shadow" to represent the less desirable side of human nature, the aspects of our character that we try to hide, reject, or ignore. Our "shadow self" is informed by repressed desires, emotions and impulses that are hidden from conscious awareness. Under certain conditions, however, this shadow self may take over and overwhelm our actions. Perhaps that's what happened to John. Despite his long history of ethical behavior—and without him even being consciously aware of them—greed, power, and the attraction of fame and glory had always been his true, if repressed, drivers.

Jung also suggested that we need to recognize the darker side of ourselves if we want to live as authentic human beings. The parts of us that we repress and deny don't just disappear. On the contrary, if they remain unexamined and unacknowledged, they may exert a degree of unconscious control over our thoughts, emotions, choices, and actions. Our shadow self may also grow more powerful and thwart our best intentions. In other words, the failure to acknowledge our shadow side is one of the biggest barriers in our journey toward living authentically. Worse, the non-integration of our shadow side can also have physical, emotional, psychological, and interpersonal consequences that can have a serious impact on our and others' lives.

John's sudden transformation, exemplified by his decision to work for a shady business tycoon, may have been his shadow side coming to the fore. Despite all his protestations, he might always have been attracted by the lifestyle of the rich and famous—the ways they had acquired their wealth be damned. At the same time, he might have preferred to remain unaware of why he was doing what he was doing. This would have required some demanding psychological acrobatics if John was going to be able to live with himself. What defense mechanisms were at work to give him some peace of mind?

When our conscience disapproves of certain actions, our way out is to find excuses to make these actions acceptable. The two main psychological defense mechanisms that John and others like him resort to are rationalization and compartmentalization. Rationalization is the process of finding a logical explanation and justification for controversial behavior or feelings, while avoiding the truth—that we have transgressed social or personal values or norms. Rationalization helps us maintain our self-respect or avoid guilt over something that, deep down, we believe is actually wrong. We try to resolve emotional conflicts by appealing to reason while obscuring our true motivation.

Compartmentalization works rather differently. When we are unable to deal emotionally with things, we put them into "compartments," dark corners of our mind where we can neatly box off issues we are unwilling to face. This helps us avoid the cognitive dissonance of having to deal with the discomfort and anxiety caused by conflicting values, emotions, and beliefs. Compartmentalization explains the kind of mental acrobatics executed by an executive who sexually harasses his female employees but behaves like a loving father to his daughters; or a senator who professes to adhere to high ethical standards while defending his president, who is a liar and philanderer. People struggling with addictions commonly entertain contradictory ideas and behaviors, and are masters in rationalization and compartmentalization, to avoid to dealing with their problem.

Unfortunately, the dark side of both rationalization and compartmentalization is that they can lead to a fracturing of the self and a divided mind. Both these defense mechanisms support and strengthen our shadow side while putting our life out of sync. Trying to manage simultaneously conflicting ways of looking at the world creates a psychological disequilibrium, which could manifest itself in troubled personal relationships, anxiety reactions (including nightmares), depression, and other forms of mental discomfort. It also leads to perceptual confusion. Someone who behaves in this manner will come across as thoughtful and considerate to some people, but nasty and out to destroy the lives of others. Not surprisingly, dealing with these people can be extremely challenging.

People like John had better keep in mind that an integrated personality is a prerequisite of mental health. To buffer the negative effects of his shadow self, John should accept and integrate these characteristics into his general personality. This means he needs to realize what's happening to him—to accept that he is behaving inconsistently or puzzlingly. He should also try to recognize and avoid the triggers, or external stimuli, that elicit the strong emotional responses that cause these alterations in attitude. Furthermore, he should learn to accept that he, like any human being, has fears and insecurities that affect his behavior, then take the next step is to overcome them. His real challenge will be to learn how to stop this process of self-deception—the urge to lie to himself. To prevent these defensive maneuvers from coming to the fore, it would help John to establish a support network of family, close friends, and others with whom he can talk and who will provide him with a better sense of reality. That might well include finding an executive coach or even a psychotherapist. If John just lets things slide, however, his "leadership brand"—which is already damaged—will be perceived as inauthentic and harm his relationships with the outside world. To maintain his sanity, John would do well to take to heart Mahatma Gandhi's statement: "Happiness is when what you think, what you say and what you do are in harmony."

10

Everything Is Bad: Complaining as a Way of Life

That I be not as those are who spend the day in complaining of headache and the night in drinking the wine which gives the headache!
—Johann Wolfgang von Goethe

Never complain and never explain.
—Benjamin Disraeli

What an earful I got when I asked Peter, an old acquaintance, how he was doing. Straightaway, he started an endless lament about everything that was wrong in his life, starting with work, his relationship with his wife, and a long list of other grievances. Given the energy he put into it, it felt like complaining had become his major pastime. After listening to Peter's moaning and groaning, I experienced a kind of visceral reaction—I felt wiped out. Peter didn't give me a chance to move beyond his cycle of negativity. Whenever I tried to reframe his situation more positively, he would respond with negativity and continue bemoaning how miserable he was. After a few minutes, I started to feel miserable myself.

I have had some experience of chronic complainers, so I know that spending time with them can be emotionally draining. I often find that many of them are unaware of the toxic impact their constant complaints and negativity have on others. Some of them even think that their complaining provides a sort of service for others by alerting them to potential problems.

I wondered whether Peter realized what he was doing. He certainly seemed unaware that his chronic complaining was tormenting and exasperating the people around him and putting considerable stress on himself. In fact, chronic complaining can be dangerous to mental well-being. The constant repetition of bad, sad, mad, and powerless feelings can "rewire" the neurotransmitters in our brain and reinforce negative thought patterns. These negative neural pathways facilitate unhappy thoughts, leaving little room for more positive feelings, like gratitude, appreciation, and well-being. A continuous cycle of negative thoughts may even damage our hippocampus, the part of the brain used for problem solving and cognitive functioning.[1] Over time, the engrained habit of chronic complaining may turn into a default behavior pattern. Complainers become negativity addicts, attracted to the drama that accompanies a complaining attitude and stirring up toxic sludge wherever they go.

Chronic complainers are also prone to black-and-white thinking. Compromise is unknown to them. They are more likely to see problems than solutions and consequently find it difficult to make decisions. Ironically, the paradox of their dysfunctional thinking is that it creates more things to complain about.

Disturbingly, listening to people's constant complaints can have a negative influence on my own thinking. In psychoanalytic psychology there is the concept of "projective identification," which occurs when negative and pessimistic people around you transfer these feelings to you, without either party realizing it. You become their garbage can and containing their negativity can make you feel weighed down and exhausted.

Interestingly, it is very likely that this kind of "transfer" is part of our evolutionary makeup. Some neuroscientists have suggested that we have what they call "mirror" neurons in our brain, which are important for our species' survival.[2] As social beings, our brains unconsciously mimic the moods of the people around us. This can be an advantage when we are faced with danger and can also serve as a form of social cohesion. However, this mirroring has a flip side. You need to be cautious about spending too much time with people who complain about everything. Before you know it, you could become a complainer too.

Why do complainers behave in this way? Why do they keep on burdening others with their complaints? What are they trying to accomplish?

One reason for complaining is that it is an opportunity to decompress. Occasional venting of negative emotions to someone else can be a form of catharsis. In fact, it is important for our mental and physical equilibrium that we are attuned to our feelings and the messages they send us. Repressing our

---

[1] https://news.stanford.edu/pr/96/960814shrnkgbrain.html.
[2] Giacomo Rizzolatti and Laila Craighero (2004). The mirror-neuron system, *Annual Review of Neuroscience*, 27, 169–192, https://doi.org/10.1146/annurev.neuro.27.070203.144230.

feelings might stop us recognizing we have a problem and getting to the bottom of it. Complaining allows us to get our concerns out into the open, and so lessens possible stress reactions.

Another reason why people complain incessantly is that they seek attention and sympathy in order to feel better about themselves. Perhaps Peter wanted me to say, "Poor you. I know how you feel. If I were in your place, I'd also be upset." It's possible that he wanted validation from me for his feelings of unfairness. Perhaps he wanted to establish emotional connection by sharing his misery.

Other, more Machiavellian, reasons behind constant complaining are manipulation and control. Complaints can be used to exercise power and influence perceptions, especially within organizations, which are hotbeds of political games and power dynamics. Mudslinging and smear campaigns are tools used to shape others' opinions. People can use complaints as part of a political strategy to canvas help in their campaigns against particular individuals or ideologies.

Thinking specifically about Peter, I wondered where his negative perceptions came from. If children learn that whining gets attention within the family, they adopt complaining as an effective but dysfunctional style of communication. Could this have been Peter's experience? Complaining might have been a way to gain visibility and establish rapport with his parents. Unfortunately, early experiences can become deeply ingrained patterns of behavior. In Peter's case, he had developed a victim mentality and his complaining mode had become part of his identity. This might explain why he reacted badly to advice—which he did—because resolving an issue would take away his reason to complain: it would threaten his sense of self.

Dealing with chronic complainers I have learned the hard way how resistant they can be to support, morale-boosting, or advice. My constructive comments often have little or no effect. I knew that whatever I would say to Peter, however much I would empathize with him, he would continue to obsess about the downside of his situation, rather than seek solutions. This is what makes dealing with chronic complainers so exasperating and why my heart sinks when I see one coming.

One strategy to handle complainers is to resort to some form of boundary management. Faced with Peter, I need to be explicit with him: I'm prepared to listen and to talk, but not to engage in a repetitive conversation. Just going over the same thing time and time again will do neither of us a service.

Peter needs to listen to and hear some hard talking. I could point out that while I recognize that he feels bad, he has become a stress projector and his constant complaining is having a negative effect on me. I could tell him that everyone complains, in moderation, without turning it into a modus operandi. I could point out that there is a right and wrong way to complain. Complaining is useful in situations where it might affect real and positive change; however, complaining without focus isn't constructive. I could tell him that he would be much better off if he could adjust his perspective and vent with a purpose. Purposeful complaining—taking a proactive stand—will give him a roadmap to transcending his negativity. After all, if he has the time to whine and complain about all the bad things happening to him, so he also would have the time to do something about them. He should be trying to fix and solve something, not just looking for sympathy.

I could also tell Peter that cultivating a sense of gratitude could help him "unlearn" his complaining habit. The urge to complain should be a red flag to shift his attention from counting his complaints to counting his blessings. He might discover that his mood improves; he will have more energy and feel less anxious. And over time, with enough practice, this positive attitude could be a new approach to life.

Of course, creating this kind of a behavior change takes time. It is a journey that can be supported by a coach or psychotherapist, someone who would work with Peter to explore why he constantly tries to seek confirmation from others, and how to work on alternative responses when he feels a need to complain.

This is important because, while chronic complainers appear to be superficially harmless, their endless and purposeless negativity can become extremely toxic. Chronic complainers like Peter owe it to themselves, and the people they work and live with, to regulate their toxic behavior. Peter would be much better off by learning to be grateful for what he has. He might come to realize that complaining depresses everyone, does him no good, and doesn't solve any problems. It is no route to a happier life. In fact, he should keep in mind that the squeaking wheel doesn't always get the grease: it can also be replaced.

11

The Belligerent (B) Personality

The thing I hate about an argument is that it always interrupts a discussion.
—Gilbert Chesterton

Man is by nature competitive, combative, ambitious, jealous, envious, and vengeful.
—Arthur Keith

Serge was in two minds about the case, Steve, a business acquaintance, was putting to him. Steve wanted him to help settle a dispute involving Steve's father, Bernard, who was determined to sue his own brother over a property they jointly owned. Steve explained to Serge that his father was notorious for suing everyone within sight—including family members. Litigation seemed to be his favorite pastime. He declared war on anybody who crossed him. Conflict was the defining factor of all his relationships. He escalated minor problems into major issues. This dysfunctional tendency was complicated by his inability to connect his actions to their consequences. Even though he was the instigator of all these dramas, he always saw himself as the victim. Someone else was always to blame.

Someone familiar with the lawsuit had told Steve that there had been many opportunities to bring it to an end. Unfortunately, for Bernard it was "nothing doing." It seemed he wanted not only to win but also to crush his brother. Negotiation toward an equitable solution to the conflict was out of the question. It was as if Bernard didn't want to come to a resolution. Instead, he resorted to self-sabotaging behavior that worsened the situation. Antagonism obviously made him feel good. Meanwhile, Steve had discovered that this wasn't the only legal suit Bernard was pursuing. His litigiousness threatened to clog up the courts with a series outrageous claims. His daily life was subsumed in urgency and drama.

Does Bernard's behavior sound familiar? Do you know people who enjoy arguing for arguing's sake? Do you meet people who can't bear to think or admit that they might be wrong? Have you encountered people who provoke and thrive on conflictual relationships?

We all have different personality characteristics—that is, enduring patterns of behavior that come to the fore in early adulthood. However, these become dysfunctional when they become too rigid and extreme and impair our behavior. Belligerent people like Steve do not fit neatly into one particular personality type or another. Their modus operandi includes elements of the antisocial (psychopathic), borderline, narcissistic, and the histrionic personality.

Like many psychiatric disorders, the specific causes of the belligerent (B) personality have not been clearly identified. There is no known genetic link for this disorder although temperament seems to play a role in its development. However, there is an association between this disorder and chaotic early family life. Abuse, neglect, and significant conflict in early childhood seem to be contributing factors. Often, child-parent attachment patterns have been disrupted. These early life experiences may produce behavior characterized by impulsivity, inappropriate or intense anger, difficulty controlling anger, unstable and intense interpersonal relationships, and a defective self-image or sense of self.

How do B types deal with the world at large? Generally speaking, their overall way of interacting involves considerable, persistent, and maladaptive aggression that can be expressed in a variety of ways and in a wide range of circumstances. Their emotional volatility can be quite intimidating. They have trust and control issues and a very dark view of human nature. In any relationship, they actively try to gain the upper hand.

At the same time, B types have a knack for portraying themselves as victims. They refuse to acknowledge that they may have contributed—in even the smallest way—to whatever conflict in which they're involved. They're extremely reluctant to take any responsibility when things go wrong. They are always right, and others are always to blame. "It's your/his/her/their fault" are their stock phrases.

Obviously, their capacity for empathy is seriously limited. It's almost impossible to get them to consider other people's points of view. Consequently, they don't recognize that they're often the authors of their own misery. To be able to stick to their position, they determinedly distort reality and equally determinedly believe that their cognitive distortions are the truth, fighting off contradictory information and preferring to convince others to see things their way.

As the example of Bernard shows, B types tend to do or say things without thinking about the potential consequences. Their negative mindset means they see threats and dangers everywhere and always see the worst in people. Minimizing the positive and maximizing the negative in every encounter makes it more likely that they will start or become involved in arguments.

B types live in a black-and-white world. People are either for them or against them. There is no middle ground. The people they deal with are perceived either as all good (over-idealized) or all bad (devalued). Given their binary way of looking at things, they are primed to do battle with anybody who stands in their way.

B types make a fuss about even the most trivial things, just to create trouble. They view conflict as a normal way of behaving and seem to thrive on it. Bernard certainly demonstrated this aspect of the B type personality. He also had a typically short fuse. People like Bernard drive other people crazy because they are almost always on the attack, even over completely insignificant things.

To further their own ends, B types actively and deliberately seek to exploit and victimize others. They can be ruthlessly self-advancing, generally at the expense of other people—and the truth. And once they are determined to have their way, it is almost impossible to get them to stop. They must win. But if they lose, they don't go down easily. If they can, they will take some of the sting out of defeat by taking others with them.

Sadly enough, B types have very little insight into their dysfunctional behavior and are generally resistant to suggestions they might change. But if they express a desire for help, several things need to be kept in mind.

The reason these people behave so antagonistically is related to feelings of low self-esteem. Their arrogant and antagonistic façade hides a great deal of fragility and vulnerability. In addition, they aren't happy. After all, being angry most of the time is no prescription for happiness.

Because these people don't feel good about themselves, they have turned their negative feelings outward (in the form of anger). They find it more convenient to zero in on the shortcomings of others than pay attention to their own. By acting this way, they avoid ever looking inside themselves to understand why they behave the way they do. Unfortunately, it is exactly this lack of self-understanding that continuously drives them into one dispute after another. It can be interpreted as a highly dysfunctional way of relating to others, but it is a pattern that they have learned in childhood.

As B types are not naturally insightful, helping them to change is always going to be an uphill struggle. They will try to divert attention from their own bad behavior whenever they can and deny their responsibility for any problematic situation. Getting them to accept that they may be part of the problem will be hard work. They will keep on finding excuses until they find people who agree with their point of view. Predictably, they think lawyers and mental health professionals make attractive "co-conspirators." After all, lawyers have to represent them, and therapists have to like them.

Knowing all this, it's little wonder Serge might hesitate about taking on Bernard as a client. If he does, he's going to have to tread very carefully when helping him change his behavior. B types are easily threatened and quick to go on the defensive. They will automatically interpret any effort to help them as an attack: would-be helpers can expect an "adult" temper tantrum if they make a comment that's not appreciated. The tendency of B types only to see the worst in people adds to the difficulty in establishing a working alliance. It isn't uncommon for helpers to become the target of their client's wrath.

Serge will also need to maintain a healthy degree of skepticism about what Bernard tells him. B types will distort information so that it fits the way they feel; in effect, their feelings create their facts. These unconscious distortions and delusions lead to conscious lying and making things up. While mental health professionals might recognize this pattern, most businesspeople and legal professionals will not understand what's going on. Consequently, they become absorbed in trying to figure out who is lying, wasting their time investigating fictional information.

However, this is looking ahead to what Serge can expect if he begins working with Bernard. Obviously, it's not going to be easy but the first hurdle—getting Bernard to the point when he looks for help—will be even harder. If B types experience enough discomfort in their current life situation, they might be prepared to seek professional help from an executive coach or psychotherapist. But even if they make that step, they can be extremely resistant to change. Given their argumentativeness, need for control and defensiveness, tackling their behavior directly and giving negative feedback will bring the change process to a rapid halt.

The most effective option is "conversational judo," using the "opponent's" own strength to create movement—in other words, to guide the conversation along in the direction the client leads it. Serge should never force his opinion on Bernard. Rather than trying to prove him wrong, he should withdraw from an argument and allow Bernard to draw his own conclusions, while providing matter-of-fact feedback about the potential consequences of the actions Bernard may be considering. He could also help him to look at other alternatives. The essential thing is to try to remain objective and resist being drawn into Bernard's binary world—the place where people are either for him or against him. He should avoid taking sides.

Despite their formidable resistance, B types can change if they are willing to explore the underlying psychological dynamics that contribute to their seemingly meaningless fights. If they can do this, they may come to realize that argumentation has become their particular way to get some form of recognition—to be noticed. They need to understand why they have exaggerated responses to seemingly minor issues; they must realize what real intrapsychic drama lies behind them. Eventually (guided by the helper), they may be able to figure it out for themselves. There may come a point when they realize the high price they're paying for this highly dysfunctional way of relating to the world.

It's important that helpers who try to deal with B types realize that while their reactions may seem incomprehensible, or even petty, they are in fact reactions to something very real but unacknowledged: past hurts. However, their emotional illiteracy results in exaggerated responses to even minor issues; they just don't understand why they are acting the way they do. Serge will have to approach his interactions with Bernard with a hefty dose of empathy.

Emphasizing their self-efficacy will help B types move forward. As an opening move, Serge could say how much he recognizes Bernard's strengths and accomplishments. This kind of reassurance can help B types build a modicum of self-confidence and encourage positivity and proactive approaches to life. At the same time, while stressing Bernard's self-efficacy, Serge should encourage him to set realistic expectations about what he can accomplish when faced with challenging situations. He should help him to stay focused on the task at hand, not to overreact and go off the deep end.

When Bernard becomes more confident, his need for argumentation and conflict is likely to abate. He may stop resorting to the defense mechanisms that have protected him emotionally in the past. There may even come a point when he realizes that these defense mechanisms have become outdated—that the time has come to replace them with more constructive ones.

Furthermore, Bernard may come to realize that truths must be addressed on both sides of a conflict. Exhausting people with a series of objections is not the same as convincing them. He should remind himself that even if he manages to "win," a conflict is not necessarily solved. Winning an argument is also losing it, as it makes the loser feel bad.

The holy grail for B types like Bernard is to recognize the need for compromise and to be prepared to do it. With the right help, they will get there; the journey might be hard and long, but it will bring great rewards.

12

Managing "On the Borderline"

Whoever fights monsters should see to it that in the process he does not become a monster.
—Friedrich Nietzsche

Everyone has wishes which he would not like to tell to others, which he does not want to admit even to himself.
—Sigmund Freud

One day, I received a FaceTime call from a business acquaintance asking me if I would be willing to help a family business to put some order in their affairs. The issue he presented was that they needed some help straightening out the governance of their family business. Afterward, thinking over our conversation, I wondered what had *not* been said during the discussion. The issues he described sounded far too easy. If they really were so straightforward, why did they need my help? Despite my misgivings, I decided I wanted to find out more and agreed to an exploratory meeting with these two family members.

It was a strange meeting. The father (I'll call him Richard) talked continuously while his son (Louis), who was sitting beside him, nodded affirmatively to everything he said. Most of Richard's talk covered business generalities and was otherwise a commentary on the long history of the company. While Richard was talking, I was struck by his self-aggrandizement—all the great things that had happened in this multi-generational company were attributed to his genius. But during his monologue, he said nothing about the future and succession. I worked out quickly that, despite his silence, it was Louis who wanted to meet me. I also sensed that his father had agreed extremely reluctantly.

I left with very mixed feelings about the meeting. That same evening, Louis contacted me through FaceTime. He wanted to know how I thought the meeting had gone but, without waiting for my answer, immediately asked if I wanted to hear the real story? Then he poured his heart out about the difficulties he had working with his father. He started by saying that he had always played the role of a "good son" and had done everything his father wanted. And he had done it well. As a matter of fact, while he was CEO, the company's sales had increased dramatically. But his father had lost touch with the business. According to Louis, Richard was too busy dealing with the many expensive "trinkets" that came with his wealth. He added that his father's recent decision to be more involved in the business, due to their deteriorating relationship, had resulted in decisions that were endangering the company's future. After this outpouring, Louis asked me if I would be willing to help him to deal with the situation by meeting his father once more to explore succession. Again, I agreed, somewhat warily, and committed myself to a date.

Very soon after this call, I received an SMS from Richard wondering why the proposed meeting was necessary. Couldn't we just have a quick phone call to get it over with? I texted him back that I thought it wasn't a good idea to deal with such important matters by phone. Clearly put out, Richard consented.

Arriving in the city where Richard lived, I was brought to his estate. After one of the servants had given me a tour of the house, the "old man" appeared and replayed his monologue about the history of the company. He reiterated what a business hero he was; how his great ideas had been the reason for the company's success; and how often he had saved the company from disaster. Most of what he said was familiar to me, as I'd read a few newspaper stories about him and his organization. However, while he was talking, I had no chance to interrupt and tell him I knew a lot of the story already. When I first tried, Richard accused me of being sarcastic, and at another point even yelled at me, saying that I talked too much. When I tried to disagree, he yelled again—so I let it go, and concentrated instead on grasping the backdrop to his behavior.

Richard's family situation didn't seem quite so rosy. He appeared to be estranged from most of his family. Bizarrely, he referred to several of his family members as "exes." Recently, his relationship with Louis, which had been very close, had also become tense. They no longer saw things the same way. But it was clear that Richard was upset by this change in their relationship. In response, I suggested that they could develop some kind of roadmap of how to move forward. At that point, Richard picked up his phone and summoned his son, who lived close by, to come to his mansion.

When Louis arrived, the conversation deteriorated very quickly. Richard accused him of keeping him uninformed. He told him that the financial information he received about the company wasn't helpful and that he didn't like the way the figures were presented. He also questioned Louis about the company's profitability and voiced concerns about liquidity issues (given his need to maintain his opulent lifestyle). He went on and on, complaining about everything that Louis had done. Finally, we made the decision to sleep on these various topics and continue our discussion the following morning.

I returned to my hotel room, but because I had difficulties sleeping thinking about the events of the previous day, I thought that it would be a good idea to present Richard with a preliminary protocol of how other family businesses handled family governance. I wrote up a simplified protocol and sent it to him that night. When I woke up the next morning and looked at my phone, I saw that Richard had sent me a series of convoluted messages. The main gist of them was my presumptuousness for sending him a family governance transition plan. He was insulted by the protocol and what he perceived were the implications: Did I want him dead? Was I trying to take the company away from him? Richard stated that it was his company, nobody else's. I was flabbergasted by his reaction to what I had thought was a rather innocuous document, like the ones I had used many times before when helping family businesses to move forward.

When I met up with Richard and Louis later that day, Richard started to yell at me, accusing me of being a liar and a fraud. Obviously, the only reason that I was there was to help his son to steal his company away from him. While Richard verbally abused me, Louis tried to calm him down, without success. Eventually, I felt the best thing to do was simply to leave. There wasn't much I could do, given Richard's state of mind.

Clearly, this assignment turned out to be far more than I had bargained for when I accepted it. On reflection, I told myself that notwithstanding his overreactions, Richard was trying to communicate something. His behavior, surrealistic though it appeared, probably made perfect sense to him. It could have been his attempt to deal with a very stressful family situation. Probably, the looming breakup with his son—the only family member he was still talking to—had been the catalyst.

People with borderline personality disorders—and who suffer from psychotic episodes—are challenged on three dimensions: reality testing, identity problems, and resorting to primitive defenses. All three were evident with Richard. His reactions were founded on his huge mistrust of those around him rather than on reality. People on the borderline are preoccupied with hidden motives, and fearful of being deceived or betrayed. Given his paranoid outlook to the world, talking to Richard was like walking on eggshells. Unfortunately, when Louis wanted to get his father to clarify succession issues, he joined the list of people Richard thought were likely to betray him.

As far as identity issues were concerned, Richard saw himself as a grandiose entrepreneur, while his understanding of the very complex business he had inherited was extremely poor. In reality, he was living the life of an aging playboy, quite out of touch with the intricacies of his business.

With respect to his use of defense mechanisms, Richard seemed to live in a paranoid world, where things were either black or white. This primitive process of "splitting" was his preferred defense mechanism: people were either for him or against him, leaving no room for nuances or compromise.

Another explanation for Richard's bewildering behavior was his inability to relax, revealed in his disorganized thoughts and speech patterns and his tendency to be extremely argumentative. Of course, as I was perceived to be in his son's camp, I had become a target for his projections.

Unfortunately, for people on the borderline there is always a "selective" reality, driven by paranoia. For Richard, this centered on money. He had falsely accused his son of trying to steal his wealth, whereas in fact Louis had made him very rich. The catalyst for the emergence of these paranoid thoughts may have been his son calling for greater transparency about the way the family office was run.

I wanted to make sense of what was happening to Richard. I saw his antics as a sad, exhausting effort by an aging, lonely man, fearful of his mortality, who was trying to maintain control over what seemed to be a very delicate mental equilibrium. Sadly enough, emotional, and cognitive disturbances like Richard's only increase over time. Psychotic episodes tend to become much more common as people get older. For some, these symptoms emerge when brain function deteriorates with age. The onset of such psychotic episodes is especially common among people who suffer from Alzheimer's Disease. Other health conditions can also interfere with brain functioning, as can some kinds of medications whose side effects may include delusions, hallucinations, or other types of psychotic reactions. During my interactions with Richard, I had noticed he was quite a pill popper. Abuse of—or withdrawal from—alcohol or other substances can also cause psychotic symptoms. Although I didn't see any evidence of alcohol abuse in Richard, I was aware that people with a history of psychosis are highly likely to have problems related to drug or alcohol abuse. These substances often provide short-term relief, although in the long term they usually worsen symptoms.

Louis wondered how he could help and support his father. Would it take some form of dramatic action? Many people were employed by the company, and Louis was afraid that his father's condition could endanger the organization's future.

Richard had been able to maintain some kind of psychological equilibrium as long as his son, who had become an extension of himself, did his bidding. Louis' desire for "individuation"—to become a person in his own right—seemed to have been the trigger that knocked Richard off balance. Louis' questions about the way the family office was run weren't appreciated and his request to put a succession plan in place—understandable, given his father's age—was seen as a major hostile act. He interpreted it that his son wanted him dead. Also, I surmised that Richard's realization that he didn't have full control over his son made him fearful of being seen as the impostor he really was. The house of cards he had built up so carefully—a "house" supported by his son—was falling apart. All these years, his son had helped him to maintain the fantasy of being a glorious, visionary, wheeler-dealer businessman.

Borderline disorders among executives aren't rare. Psychotic episodes tend to be more common than most of us realize. The question is, how should we deal with them? Diagnosis is one thing, but treatment is a very different matter.

In a few cases, in the context of family-controlled businesses, family members may resort to extreme measures. For example, a CEO I knew recounted how, at one point in his life, his family members had "kidnapped" him through forced hospitalization, fearful that his erratic behavior was endangering the future of the company. The excuse his family members had given to the outside world was that he was suffering from burnout. In his case, the hospitalization worked. After a short period of time, he returned to his position as CEO. However, this man was much younger than Richard. Also, unlike Richard, he had a very supportive wife who helped him during and after this transition period. Louis was not likely to resort to involuntary commitment unless Richard made decisions that put himself or others in real danger.

Unfortunately, there isn't a "cure" for Richard's psychotic episodes. However, there are various treatment options that could help ameliorate his condition. In his case, antipsychotic medication could be prescribed, in combination with psychotherapy and other forms of social support.

However, I thought it highly unlikely that Richard would agree to such an intervention. Given the way psychotic disorders affect the brain, the individuals affected often fail to recognize what's happening to them. In fact, most people who experience psychotic episodes are very reluctant to enter treatment, fearful of its effects on their mental and physical state—with some reason, as it is difficult to predict the efficacy of antipsychotic medication. There can be significant cognitive and physical side-effects to these drugs, including blurred vision, restlessness, drowsiness, stiffness, trembling, constipation, and even sexual dysfunction. Finding the right medication always necessitates a trial-and-error period, again something I couldn't imagine Richard embracing.

I couldn't foresee a happy ending for Richard. Obviously, I hadn't been effective in giving advice. In terms of creating behavior change my impact had been negligible. However, without having been able to build some kind of "working alliance" it would have been impossible to reach Richard's more "rational" self. When I expressed my willingness to take on the assignment, I had no idea how serious the case was going to be. In hindsight, I don't think I ever had a chance.

Without a dramatic intervention, which would require Louis to overtly challenge his father and stage a coup, Richard was going to run his company into the ground. I hoped that the professional management team would be able to act as a buffer when Richard went off the rails, although it seemed doubtful: they didn't have the same influence that Louis had.

Louis was faced with several scenarios, none of them attractive. Whatever decision he made, he was in for a difficult time. Completely breaking his ties with his father was going to be a real challenge.

From the perspective of his own mental health, the best thing I could advise Louis to do was to take some distance from the situation, which he did. He decided to take a leave of absence even though he knew this might endanger his newly created executive top team. Time off would give him space to start rebuilding his own life.

However, Louis was concerned that if he distanced himself completely, his father would be financially exploited by the people with whom he had surrounded himself. For example, one of the concerns Louis had raised with his father was the inadequate checks and balances in the family office. When he had pointed this out, it became one of the "hot potatoes," and received aggressive push back from Richard's advisors. Louis suspected that something unwholesome was going on. What were they trying to hide?

Considering this, Louis decided to maintain some kind of relationship with his father, while also protecting his own mental health. Even though he was taking some distance, remaining present would enable him to see how events evolved.

Louis' challenge would be to stay as non-judgmental as possible, which would not be easy, given Richard's volatile emotional state. But if he was to be able to maintain some kind of relationship with his father, he needed to avoid criticizing or blaming him for his actions. He would need to remember that there were logical explanations behind his father's psychotic episodes, illogical as they appeared.

Attempts to argue with his father using reason and logic would be futile and a waste of time. Instead of directly attacking his father's defenses, he would need to disarm him by listening to what he had to say, while reassuring him that he appreciated what Richard had achieved.

Louis shouldn't take personally the accusations his father threw at him: these outbursts were expressions of Richard's disordered thinking. Caught between his dependency on his son—one of his last meaningful relationships—and his loneliness, fear of aging, and of letting go, Richard's inner world was full of demons.

Finally, whatever situation he found himself in, Louis should try to stay positive and supportive. He should keep his head up and be patient. But in all his interactions with his father, he should try to maintain a level of detachment, given his father's unconscious attempts to drive him crazy. I was left feeling that my only effective contribution was to have been able to reframe this very difficult situation in a positive way: his father's breaking point had become Louis' own turning point. It had become his opportunity for a reset.

13

How to Support People Struggling with Poor Mental Health?

Not until we are lost, do we begin to understand ourselves.
—Henry David Thoreau

Life doesn't make any sense without interdependence. We need each other, and the sooner we learn that, the better for us all.
—Erik Erikson

Recently, when I visited one of my clients, he told me the following story. A month previously, one of his colleagues showed up for work looking extremely distressed. Everyone felt he was acting strangely. As soon as he reached his office, he began to empty his desk. In the process, he gave several small, beautiful art objects that decorated his office to one of his assistants. While he was busily doing all these things, nobody had the courage to ask him why. The next day he didn't show up for work. When an assistant called him on his cell and at home there was no response. People at the office knew very little about him, apart from the fact that he lived alone and had been divorced for some time. When there was no sign of him the day after, they started to worry. Realizing that something was very wrong, they contacted his daughter. When she let herself into her father's house, she found his body. He had killed himself.

My client told me that, afterward, many people in the organization felt guilty for not having recognized, or even ignored, the warning signs that their colleague was in mental distress. His suicide had impacted not only his loved ones, but also many people in the organization. His fellow executives felt that they should have been much more alert to what had been going on. But instead of dealing with the discomfort of this person's strange behavior, they opted to bury their heads in the sand.

This story is an extreme case, but many people find it difficult to talk about mental health, in either a private or an organizational setting. They don't realize that failing to pay attention to employees' mental health can be very costly. The total productivity costs of absenteeism due to mental distress are staggering. Nevertheless, the stigma associated with bringing the issue to the fore persists in many workplaces. Many employers are unaware, however, how widespread mental health problems really are. And even if they recognize it as a problem, they don't know how to deal with it. Discussing people's mental state is fraught with taboos, with predictable consequences: employees are not getting the help and support they need.

Resorting to denial—not wanting to see that there is a problem—is not the answer. For too long, we have swept the topic of mental illness under the carpet, hoping that it will just go away. But given the omnipresence of mental health issues, we need much more openness, transparency and understanding in dealing with them.

According to the latest data from the World Health Organization, one in four people in the world will be affected by a mental health issue at some point in their life, and anxiety disorders, depression, substance abuse and suicide are at the top of the WHO list.[1] Mental ill health can range from feeling "a bit down" or common symptoms like anxiety and depression, to more severe and rarer conditions, such as psychotic episodes, bipolar disorders or schizophrenia. I should add, however, that the percentage of mental disorders varies by country, with the US having the highest rates, probably due to a greater cultural willingness to report them. In many other countries, people are more hesitant to admit to these kinds of problems, contributing to their underestimation. In other countries, mental illness is completely taboo, and cases are ignored.

Although a wide variety of treatments is available, nearly two-thirds of people with known mental health issues never seek help from a health professional, mostly due to the stigma attached to doing so. Many people view suffering from a mental health issue as a personal failure. They feel embarrassed, and afraid that others may think they are crazy. Also, they may find it difficult to explain what's going on inside them, especially if they don't understand it themselves. No wonder so many are unwilling to face what's really going on.

---

[1] https://www.who.int/whr/2001/media_centre/press_release/en/.

13 How to Support People Struggling with Poor Mental Health?

Unlike physical illnesses or disabilities, mental health problems are not visible. This might be seen as a comparative advantage, as someone suffering from mental illness is unlikely to be subjected to open discrimination. But it is far from advantageous. If other people don't realize what is going on, a sufferer will not get the support that's needed.

Most of us will experience a diagnosable mental health issue at some point in our life. Hardly anybody is without some kind of mental health issue, whether it's depression, anxiety, or difficulty dealing with relationships. Even if we aren't directly affected ourselves, members of our family, or someone we know, will be. All of us will be touched by mental illness, not least because mental health and physical health are closely connected. If we are physically sick—if, for example, we have cancer—people will pay attention. But mental illness is a very different ballgame because of the loneliness and alienation it can create. It is ironic that we live in a world where, when we break a limb, everyone rushes to sign the cast, but when we are depressed, everyone runs in the opposite direction.

Of course, we must realize that there is no such thing as normal when it comes to mental health and mental illness. Mental health is a continuum, and our position on it can be anywhere. What's more, mental health is not a destination; it's a process that needs continuous attention.

From an organizational perspective, those in charge of organizations need to understand the risks posed by poor mental health and the enormous costs of mental illness in the form of reduced productivity. Mental illness is one of the most common causes of workplace absence. Conversely, they should recognize that employees with good mental health are more likely to work productively, interact better with their colleagues, have a good attendance level, and make a valuable contribution to the workplace.

The earlier a mental health issue is detected, diagnosed and treatment begins, the better off a sufferer will be. However, diagnosis is not always easy. Generally speaking, we tend to notice big or sudden changes in people while missing gradual changes in behavior. This isn't helped by the fact that many people who experience mental health issues are unwilling to reveal what's happening to them, even to their close friends and family. A red flag should go up, however, when we can observe any of the following behaviors:

- significant mood changes
- paranoid reactions/being distrustful of others
- withdrawal from other people
- appearing confused
- a deterioration in work output, motivation level and focus

- difficulties in making decisions/getting organized/finding solutions to problems
- appearing tired or anxious, losing interest in activities and tasks that previously seemed to be enjoyable
- changes in eating habits and appetite
- substance abuse.

If we think someone has mental health issues, there are several things we can do. The absolute best plan of action is to help the person seek out high-quality psychological and medical professionals. Treatment may include a combination of medication, psychotherapy, advice about healthy living and, most importantly, helping people with mental health issues learn how to help themselves. The treatment for each person will be unique—there is no set formula that works for everyone. But whatever is done, it is important for the person who is troubled to realize that seeking help is a sign of strength—not of weakness.

A common initial reaction to a diagnosis of a mental health issue is denial: "This can't be happening to me. Mental health problems happen to other people." This is a response to the generalized stigma around mental illness, the loss of self-belief and self-blame. Close family members may also blame themselves and feel responsible for not having seen it coming. But, as said before, no one is immune to mental illness. It isn't a moral weakness or a character flaw. Neither is it a life sentence. Many people with mental health issues learn to cope with the symptoms and to minimize their impact on day-to-day life.

Given the long-term investment organizations make in their human capital, their leadership needs to take a proactive stand vis-à-vis mental health issues. They should send clear signals to employees that their mental health matters to them, and that they value them as people, not as cogs in a machine. But this kind of communication is only going to be believable if the leadership of an organization has created a transparent, safe, and supportive culture, making it easier for employees to open up to their managers if they feel that something is wrong with them. There should be a clear safety net that enables employees to discuss these kinds of problems. Also, well publicized communication channels need to be in place for employees to be able to raise the topic of mental health. Everyone in the organization should know that prompt, positive action will be taken when help is asked for.

In my experience, organizations that deal with mental health issues head-on usually have considerable awareness of this subject, including problems with substance abuse. In such organizations, top management ensures that there is a zero-tolerance policy for discrimination based on a person's mental health status. Nobody should be fearful of not being treated fairly. Clear policies should be in place around sickness absence. In these organizations, employees are treated equally whether their sickness absence is for a mental or physical health problem. The company policy is to support recovery, whatever the cause of the illness.

The acid test is the way employers handle people's sickness absence and their return to work. This may include some form of flex time, job restructuring, a more accommodating work environment, or even a change of direct report to someone with a different leadership style. Actually, there will be occasions when rather than suggesting a leave of absence, it will be more effective to develop a plan that enables people with mental health issues to stay at work. Being able to be remain productive, in a supportive environment, can speed up recovery.

Of course, in some instances, it is not our personal mental health that's the problem, it's our surroundings. It may be the workplace that's driving us crazy. The concept of mental health in society is very much determined by the degree to which we fit into a system without showing signs of stress. Putting it more dramatically, there are times when the only appropriate response to an unbearable reality is to go insane.

The boisterous anti-war film *King of Hearts*, directed by Philippe de Broca in 1966, tells how, during World War I, a Scottish soldier is sent on a mission to a village in the French countryside to disarm a bomb left by the retreating German army. He encounters a strange town occupied by the former residents of the local psychiatric hospital who have escaped after the villagers deserted the place. They warmly welcome their new visitor as their King of Hearts. Gradually, the soldier starts to prefer the acceptance of the insane locals over the insanity of the war raging outside. It is a moral tale that the people who lead organizations would be wise to take to heart.

14

What Is This Person Really Telling Me?

> *The world is satisfied with words, few care to dive beneath the surface.*
> —Blaise Pascal
>
> *All art is at once surface and symbol. Those who go beneath the surface do so at their peril.*
> —Oscar Wilde

Not so long ago, I had a meeting with an executive who wondered if I could help with what he described as a very simple leadership issue in his company. I asked him, "If it is so simple, why bother, and why me?" He responded that it's sometimes useful to get a fresh pair of eyes to look at an issue. He had done some research and reckoned I would be the best person for the job. "Flattery is all right as long as you don't inhale," I reminded myself—sensibly, because he went on to say that several premier consulting firms had been unsuccessful in solving the issue. So much for his simple leadership problem!

Now, I see myself as a lot of things but not a miracle worker. It would be nice to be one, but if you want miracles, you'd better go somewhere else. When I asked him to tell me a few things about the organization, his gave me a rambling monologue about the company's ethics and how important it was to work for a value-driven organization where the leadership team really set the example. I couldn't agree more. But something wasn't right. He didn't like me trying to interrupt his account to ask questions and he kept repeating himself. What was I missing? Whatever it was, the guy was clearly a man on a mission.

He did indeed present what troubled him about the organization and the people in charge as a simple problem. I thought, however, that his comments were oversimplified. There was too much "splitting" going on. He described the people in the company as either "good" or "bad." And then there was his body language. He had a hard time making eye contact. Also, his posture was strange—stiff, unnatural. I have learned from experience that people with hidden agendas are always on edge. I have also seen how they can become frantic or over emotional at anything that derails them from their ultimate purpose. I started to ask myself what was *not* being said.

Our interchange left me with an unpleasant aftertaste. I have always been a strong believer in gut feelings; I consider intuition as another form of reasoning. It is the way your unconscious is trying to tell you something. In this instance, I didn't have the warm feeling I should get after talking to someone who feels genuine. The whole conversation had felt somewhat unreal. What wasn't he telling me? Was he disguising the real issue? What could the story behind the story be? How was the leadership really behaving? And—strange as it may sound—could he even be obscuring the real story from himself? Was the story he told me not the real story but a cover story to obfuscate what really was going on? Was he trying to use me in some way or another?

When I checked up on this value-driven company, I discovered that the major shareholder had been involved in several ethical mishaps, ending up in very contested court cases. I decided this was not the kind of client I wanted to work with.

This wasn't the first time I had been a participant in a strange conversation. Far too often, I have listened to stories that, in hindsight, seemed unreal. Consciously or unconsciously, people can embed the real story in another story. These kinds of conversations are actually part and parcel of everyday life: people have hidden agendas, meaning that the reasons we do what we do or say what we say aren't openly admitted or even known. It's like the conscious mind isn't ready to deal with the issue at hand.

For example, when I open the C-suite seminar that I give every year at INSEAD, I ask each of the participants why they are there. I sometimes put the question as "What are your crazy fantasies about being here?" Usually, the responses I get are platitudes, typically "to become a more effective leader," "to be more productive in running my teams," "to be better at culture management," "to learn how to adjust to the rapid growth of the organization"—and so on. Often, however, their real reasons for joining the workshop may have to do with their search for meaning; the sense of being stuck in their job; of being bored with what they are doing; loneliness; the feeling that their relationships with their partner and children have come to a dead end; and other existential concerns. Initially, it takes a lot of effort to bring these concerns to the surface and find the real reasons behind the reasons they give me for being there.

To some extent, we all behave like this—we tell stories, we make statements or present ourselves in a particular way, in order to make a positive impression. The reality of how we feel might be quite different, however. It is fair to say that all relationships have hidden agendas or unexpressed expectations—and this applies to marital, familial, social, political, business and virtually every other relationship. Often, we don't come out and say straightforwardly what our agenda is. We may even not be consciously aware of this agenda. Most of us do not like talking about our insecurities. Instead, we prefer to claim how tough we are, how qualified we are to do what we are doing, and even—externalizing our concerns—how idiotic other people can be.

Unfortunately, if we always have ulterior motives, if we continuously tell diverging stories, disguising what's really troubling us, we are engaged in a form of distancing. And if we stick to these kinds of dialogues, they can have a serious impact on our ability to be close to the people around us. Although having hidden agendas can serve a purpose, at times, getting stuck in them will isolate us from other people. It will interfere with our ability to really connect with others. And, in an organization, it will have an important impact on the trust equation.

The reason that our agendas may be hidden is because—at times—we aren't able or courageous enough to articulate what we really want. These dysfunctional narratives occur if we are incapable of dealing with our vulnerabilities openly and honestly. We learn to present a false persona. In other words, it is a defensive posture. Instead of directing questions inward—trying to deal with our difficulties in a more direct way—we focus our attention outward as a way of avoiding distress. Hidden agendas often represent dysfunctional interpersonal dynamics. If we dig deeply, we might find that the agenda we're hiding is caused by factors like anxiety about rejection, the fear of being seen as incompetent, greedy, power hungry, or being a control freak. With this sense of insecurity hovering in the background, we try to make ourselves feel better by disguising the real issues.

In any interpersonal exchange, we need to be attuned to the possibility that the person we're dealing with may have a hidden agenda. The challenge is how to unmask that agenda and address the real issues. But obviously, people don't display their hidden agenda—that's why it's called hidden. We need to figure it out for ourselves. And if we don't, it can become quite costly.

In any interpersonal exchange in which you're asked for advice, you should start to think about hidden agendas if you have the following reactions:

- You begin to wonder what's not being said.
- You're being seen as a messiah.
- There is too much flattery in the interchange.
- Someone seems to be trying to charm their way into your life.
- Someone is trying to tell you what they think you'd like to hear.
- You become concerned about the other person's body language.
- You have the gut feeling that something is not quite right.
- When you start to question whether perception is reality.

Too many hidden agendas will kill business effectiveness. When real issues are not addressed, hidden agendas will dominate, and performance will suffer. People will start to play by the rules of the hidden agenda instead of keeping things simple and sticking to the problem at hand. For example, I remember one CEO who asked me if I could help him in executing what he called an "Audit of Improvement." However, I discovered soon that his real agenda was wanting to fire several people at head office. What he described as a need to streamline the operations was really a request to have somebody else do the dirty work of getting rid of some people—individuals he didn't like.

Hidden agendas inhibit people from being open and honest with each other, preventing the kinds of conversations needed to help the organization move forward. And in particular, hidden agendas destroy trust. When hidden agendas prevail, it soon becomes every person for him or herself, looking out for their own best interests rather than the interests of the whole. And although people don't intentionally undermine the success of the organization, when hidden agendas prevail, that's exactly what happens. Individual motives become questionable. People's actions become self-serving. Subsequently, the morale of the company goes down the drain, endangering its future.

If hidden agendas are the modus operandi in your organization, it's time to ask yourself if they are helping you to get what you want, or if they are interfering with your ability to connect to others. Instead of resorting to hidden agendas, a better approach would be to have honest and direct conversations, with real listening on both sides. This is the way to build a culture of trust and authenticity. Perhaps, organizational authenticity may seem a hard concept to grasp, but it is built on the same foundations as individual authenticity: being honest with yourself and with others; having the ability to look inside yourself; having the courage to leave off your "armor"; not needing to be always right. It implies getting over hurt feelings rather than resorting to spitefulness and vindictiveness. It implies compassion, respect, and empathy—essential tools for self-discovery and understanding others. And, especially, if we want to free ourselves from our self-created psychic prisons, we must have the courage to be vulnerable.

In genuine conversations, we should be prepared to present our vulnerable self, to acknowledge existing emotional realities, to address painful situations, and to limit our defensiveness. In more than one way, we should try to leave our defences at the door. We should also stop splitting our world into "us" versus "them." If we are prepared to take these kinds of actions, we may discover that apparently unsolvable issues quickly shrink down to their proper proportions and can be dealt with easily.

Of course, certain manipulative personality types are more likely to have hidden agendas and not be what they appear to be. We should be on guard against people with narcissistic and antisocial personality characteristics who lack empathy, show little concern for others and are always looking out for number one. In any relationship, you'd better keep in mind that there can be occasions when the person you're willing to take a bullet for is also the one holding the gun. Always remember that an open enemy is better than a false friend and the only way to deal with toxic individuals is to refuse to play. As the saying goes, don't wrestle with a pig. You'll both get dirty, but the pig will enjoy it.

15

Are You Working in a Trust-Based Organization?

It is better to suffer wrong than to do it, and happier to be sometimes cheated than not to trust.
—Samuel Johnson

The palace is not safe when the cottage is not happy.
—Benjamin Disraeli

Recently, I spoke to a CEO who expressed shock about the level of trust in his organization. He had commissioned a survey on his organization's health. One of the questions was about the willingness of his people to speak up. To the great surprise of the CEO and the members of his executive team, more than 80 percent of the people who worked in his company said that they were reluctant to speak their mind. They felt it wasn't safe to express their opinions, doubts, or frustrations. Sadly, I had to tell this particular CEO that his organization wasn't an outlier. In many organizations, paranoia is common and trust missing, contributing to strong feelings of disengagement. The lack of trust in an organization, it is like our blood pressure. It is silent and invisible but vital to our health. This chapter explores the characteristics of low-trust versus high-trust organizations. It gives a number of recommendations of how to build a high-trust organizational culture.

I told the CEO that I often ask people in organizations the following questions:

- When you make a mistake in your organization, is it discussable?
- Are you afraid of getting into trouble (or being fired) when you speak your mind?
- Is trust a rare commodity in your organization?
- When a mistake is made in your organization, is there a tendency to shift the blame?
- Is giving candid feedback in your organization risky?
- Do you believe it's dangerous to disagree with your boss?
- Do you feel comfortable working with your colleagues?
- Do you feel often stressed out?
- Is "don't rock the boat" a common feeling in your organization?
- Are people in your organization reluctant to express their ignorance about specific matters?

If people respond affirmatively to most of these questions, their organization is more likely to be low on the trust equation and high on paranoia. The glue that holds any relationship together is trust. If that's not present, people will feel unsafe and afraid to stick their neck out.

Unfortunately, lack of trust, as my unhappy CEO found, is not obvious. The level of trust in an organization is like our blood pressure. It is silent and invisible but vital to our health. And if it is not watched carefully, it can be deadly. However, when I tell top management that they may have created a toxic work environment, they tend to become quite defensive.

A toxic work environment will be a hostile place to work. Lack of trust threatens employees' sense of self and security. In such an environment, they can, at any time, be accused of being ignorant, incompetent, or disruptive. They may be ridiculed, rejected, blamed, disrespected, intimidated, or disregarded. Also, they know they might be punished with negative performance appraisals, unfavorable work assignments or reduced promotion prospects. When this kind of organizational climate prevails, decisions aren't made, ideas aren't shared, and no employee feels comfortable working with others. Predictably, when this kind of corporate culture prevails, there will be lower employee motivation and engagement, and lower overall organizational effectiveness.

In contrast, within high-trust organizations, people know that they have voice—that they can express their opinions. What's more, they will feel more comfortable raising difficult issues, concerns and problems and offering dissenting views. They will be more willing to propose "crazy" ideas—to try something new. They also know that they will be treated fairly and respectfully. In such a safe environment, they are more prepared to express their vulnerabilities, ask for help when they need it, seek feedback, and admit to

15 Are You Working in a Trust-Based Organization?

errors or a lack of knowledge. Setbacks are considered part of the learning process. Furthermore, when employees feel that they are trusted and have the room to fail—when they believe that they will not be exposed to psychological threats—they will be much more committed and will have a greater sense of ownership. In the absence of fear and retribution, they can be more collaborative, share information and communicate openly—behaviors that will make for better team dynamics. Stress levels are also lower in such organizations. As a result, high-trust organizations will have a more productive workforce, better employee morale, and higher employee retention, also performing better from a financial perspective than their industry peers.

If trust increases profitability and helps to attract and keep talent, then it follows that a lack of trust lowers productivity and increases employee turnover. And yet despite the benefits of a high trust environment, trust remains a rare commodity in most organizations. Sadly enough, it is easier to build distrustful than trustful environments. And while it can take years to build trust, it takes only seconds to destroy it. Companies that take trust seriously, however, regularly assess their organization's culture. In these organizations, trust is always a major topic of discussion.

One of the foundations of trust is to create a community feeling within the organization. To make this happen, employees need to be aligned with the organization's purpose; they need be inspired by company values that they can understand and internalize. Senior management's alignment of words and actions will be key to building trust in the workplace. It will also be important to ensure that the values and goals of the organization's employees converge and that they match each other's expectations. As people are often poorly informed about organizational goals, top management would be wise to build a culture of transparency, keeping their employees in the loop. To get the extra mile out of their people, they also need to imbue the company's mission with meaning. As the saying goes, people work for money but die for a cause. Fair process should also be an intrinsic part of the corporate culture, ensuring that employees are treated fairly, regardless of their position within the organization.

It cannot be said strongly enough that this kind of trust building should start at the top. The organization's leadership needs to be the trendsetter. To quote the sixth-century philosopher Lao Tzu, "He who doesn't trust enough will not be trusted." People at the top need to be credible. If they say leadership development is important but fail to develop their own people, they are not believable. Thus, it is essential that an organization's leadership is dependable, consistent, keep their promises and follow through on their commitments. As so often in life, actions speak louder than words.

Trust is also built when senior management owns up to not having all the answers. Of course, it is important that senior executives have authority and know what they're talking about, but it is equally important that they admit their lack of knowledge when appropriate. Top management should be prepared to show their vulnerabilities, acknowledge their own mistakes, and encourage a culture of dialogue and accountability. Generally speaking, the willingness to take ownership of a team's failures as well as its successes is a great way to develop trust.

The way senior management deals with feedback is another important theme in the trust equation. Feedback should be a two-way street, as both giving and asking for feedback requires a lot of trust. To facilitate this exchange, an effort needs to be made to reduce hierarchy. Senior management should be open to receiving feedback from people at other levels in the organization. But in low-trust organizations, there is a reluctance to do this, as employees feel uncomfortable sharing constructive feedback with one another, let alone with their boss.

A factor of great importance in building a high-trust culture is praising people when praise is due. In particular, senior management should show appreciation and acknowledgement for a job well done. Public recognition has an enormous trust-building effect. The flipside to this is avoiding blaming and shaming. In trust-based organizations there is minimal "office gossip." Rumor and gossip are like cancer in the workplace: they can destroy the morale of an organization.

Top management should also show that they are interested in the development of their people. They should invest in their employees' personal growth and career path and not look at them as money-making machines. Executives who walk this line of talk have a competitive advantage over those that don't make the effort.

For organizations that want to attract and retain the best people and achieve the best results, a trust-based culture is not optional. Entry to the organization is a critical juncture, so top management needs to pay attention to the onboarding process. They need to assess the likely "fit" of newcomers and make them feel welcome. If this process is done properly, it will have a very positive effect on employee retention. Senior management that's interested in building high-trust organizations and engaged places to work would be wise to work on their soft skills and apply some of the actions described here.

16

Co-leadership: A Curse or a Blessing?

Coming together is a beginning; keeping together is progress; working together is success.
—Henry Ford

It is amazing what you can accomplish when you do not care who gets the credit.
—Harry Truman

Leonard, the chairman of a global consumer product company, was wondering what to do with the two co-CEOs running the company. Originally, it had seemed a great idea to have two highly complementary individuals run the company after the unexpected resignation of their predecessor for health reasons. The reality, however, was a failed dyad characterized by an extremely conflictual relationship, unclear decision-making processes, stalled initiatives, and an overall lack of direction—in other words, complete organizational drift. The dysfunctional leadership was echoed by the departure of some of the company's most valued executives.

Leonard knew when he put the co-leadership structure in place, that as an organizational design, it was relatively rare in the business world. Even if he hadn't known it, several of his peers wasted no time in pointing it out to him. They warned that co-leadership could be an open invitation to destructive power-struggles, conflict over strategic decisions, and blurred accountability. But Leonard remained a strong advocate for co-leadership. He used the health sector as an example, where dyadic structures—usually made up of one person with medical expertise and the other with administrative skills—seemed to work relatively well. The configuration seemed to help the co-leaders strengthen interorganizational synergies as well as deal with the increasing complexity of the world in which they were operating. Also, co-leadership was not unusual in both professional service and family firms.

However, Leonard's peers appeared to have been right. The problems they anticipated were clearly now visible in the company. What had gone wrong?

Despite the risks that accompany it, there are good reasons for setting up a shared leadership design in the board room. Co-leadership is about more than just the two people who spearhead an organization. A shared leadership model concentrates attention on the relational and collaborative aspects of work, as well as the ways in which the value of relationships can be incorporated into an organization's leadership structures.

Having a leadership dyad enables two people to combine their capabilities and energies to lead in a unique, constructive way and surpass what each might accomplish individually. And if they're prepared to challenge and support each other, this can contribute to more creative and better-quality strategic solutions.

Another advantage of a co-leadership design is that each co-leader can take on different roles when necessary. Each leader will have a natural propensity to lead in a particular way. Combining different styles can result in leadership complementarity, with dualities like good cop/bad cop, optimist/pessimist, holistic/atomistic thinking, and other juxtapositions. When co-leadership functions well, these opposing dualities can be mutually supportive rather than conflictual, making for better decisions.

Running an organization is also a highly stressful endeavor. With a co-leadership structure, the work of each CEO can be divided, which in turn can mitigate each individual's level of stress. Shared responsibility also distributes the risk of isolation and other challenges that top executives face.

Finally, on a wider level, co-leadership can be a powerful enabler of a collaborative culture, setting in motion a dynamic that will cascade down to the rest of the organization. Having a healthy, high-performing co-leadership structure sets an example to the rest of the organization on how to share responsibilities and work with one another.

However, as Leonard discovered the hard way, merely creating co-leadership positions does not guarantee that they will work. Dyadic success very much depends on a delicate dance between leadership personality, corporate culture, and national culture. It is also important to create clarity around the rationale for co-leadership, not only for the sake of the leadership pair but also for all the other stakeholders in the company. In other words, there must be an organizational culture that understands and supports co-leadership.

Having two points of contact can be very powerful, but only if everybody is crystal clear about who is doing what. Simply assigning roles to the leadership pair will not be enough. With two people in charge, other people in the organization can be unsure whom to approach when there are problems. An important part of a leadership developmental effort is the education of the rest of the organization about this form of organizational design. Each organizational participant should be very familiar with the co-leaders' roles and responsibilities, their reporting relationships, and who should be approached with what issues. Explicitly defining role descriptions with the other executives will create realistic, practical expectations that will contribute to the success of co-leadership. Although it may lead to more informed choices, as an organizational design co-leadership isn't necessarily seamless. Finalizing a decision requires healthy debate between the co-leaders, a process that can become extremely time-consuming and long-drawn-out. Even if both leaders have a solid relationship, disagreements between the two of them will be inevitable. At times, cooperation will be difficult. Narcissistic behavior may also rear its ugly head, with power struggles coming to the fore. But if neither will budge to reach a compromise, it will result in resentment and stalled progress on a project. Dyads can also be unstable—and they easily fall apart.

Fortunately, there are some helpful guidelines for creating effective co-leadership structures. A sine qua non will be to recruit wisely. A successful pairing starts with a careful process to pick the right people. The key selection criteria should go beyond required technical expertise to consider the person/culture fit with each other and the organization. An effective complementary dyad will need established ground rules, so several important *structural* and *interpersonal measures* need to be put in place to make this kind of design work.

Structural measures:

- *Mission/vision/core values* For the co-leaders, a shared mission and vision will be critical for organizational success. Both need to buy into the organization's values. Culture compatibility is essential. The personality of each needs to fit the prevailing company culture.
- *Role definition* Clarity of roles and defined decision-making processes are imperative. The organizational structure, reporting relationships, and expected roles and responsibilities need to be clearly defined. Each co-leader needs to have an explicit delineation of his or her individual responsibility. Without this, not only will there be role confusion between the co-leaders but also the risk of confusion among other members of the organization. Accordingly, all organizational members need to be familiar with

the dyad as a joint leadership team, with complementary roles, that is jointly accountable for the organization's performance.

- *Accountability* Both co-leaders need to be held accountable for specific, measurable goals—some shared, some separate, but always complementary. In addition, given the complexity of a co-leadership structure, ongoing monitoring of accountabilities and results is needed. A co-leadership structure involves a division of the work that needs to be done, but it also opens an opportunity for each member of the dyad to shirk accountability. In situations of co-leadership, it will always be easy to blame the other when things go wrong. Each person's accountability is therefore non-negotiable.
- *Authority* Each co-leader should have sufficient latitude and power to make critical decisions and enact whatever changes they think are necessary. They should be able to make decisions in the areas for which they are accountable.

Putting these structural measures in place will be quite challenging. Most important, however, are the interpersonal processes that will make co-leadership work. In addition to technical skills, soft skills will be critical. Soft skills are often intangible and hard to quantify, but they're important for a successful co-leadership relationship.

Interpersonal measures:

- *Know thyself* Co-leaders need to be familiar with their own strengths and weaknesses. If they are incapable of recognizing their weaknesses and counter-productive behavior, they might be prone to prideful and defensive reactions. Conversely, when co-leaders are aware of their weaknesses, they will be able to build more balanced relationship dynamics that support the de-escalation of conflict toward more effective collaboration.
- *Collaboration* Given that there are two people steering the ship, co-leaders need to be able to collaborate with each other effectively. That means they should be willing to share responsibilities, make joint decisions, and generally speaking, to work well together without a high degree of conflict. However, the ability to do this will require a degree of agreeableness. Of course, as in all relationships, a degree of conflict is to be expected, but the appropriate structural arrangements and a cooperative attitude will enable conflicts to be addressed constructively. In case of contentious issues, however, the co-leaders should keep in mind that they need to be available to other people in the organization as a united pair. If they have ever been parents, they will understand the importance of taking such a stand. In parenting situations, it is well-known that conflicting responses only create

confusion. In leadership situations, when a decision requires the input of both parties, they need to be jointly available to discuss issues or risk slowing the business down.

- *Communication* It is essential that co-leaders are willing to share knowledge openly. Clear and transparent communication with each other and the organization is indispensable. Sadly, some executives believe that knowing more than the other person will strengthen their power base. Although there may be some truth to this notion, hoarding knowledge invites disaster. For co-leadership to be successful, each member of the dyad needs to share information openly and always keep the co-leader in the loop.
- *Honesty* Co-leadership implies that no single person will be making all the decisions. Both parties not only need to be transparent with each other about challenges, successes, and updates, but also need to be upfront with other people in the organization. They need to remain open to other opinions that might help get things done. A "my way or the highway" approach to decision-making will only lead to conflict. In addition, co-leaders need to be open about their failures as well as their successes. Open discussions about possible problems will provide an opportunity for mutual support and finding the best way to bounce back. Wins and losses can be discussed as a part of a weekly team meeting or in regular team retrospectives.
- *Trust* A co-leadership team works best when both leaders have a trust-based relationship. Both need to show respect and give thought to the other's position. A major tenet of a mutually valued relationship is the presence of a safe space where both partners can freely express their thoughts. A high degree of psychological safety within the dyad will facilitate mutual feedback and understanding. It will create a fertile ground for sharing knowledge, enable suggestions for improvements, and help to explore new avenues in the organization. Without trust, feelings of insecurity and anxiety will thrive and, each co-leader will waste time and energy on monitoring the other's motives and behavior, sabotaging the success and morale of the overall organization.

Often, to make a co-leadership structure work, executive coaching is needed to help leaders fit appropriately into their roles. Constant monitoring will be needed to see if the co-leadership design still works. Left to their own devices, there is always a chance that the pair might devolve into separate worlds and the leadership relationship will become dysfunctional.

Co-leadership will be a constant learning exercise because shared responsibilities contribute to greater complexity. It will always be an uphill challenge to make it work. But experience has shown that when it does, co-leadership can make for a truly high-performance organization.

17

Onboarding or Unboarding?

Choose a job you love and you will never have to work another day in your life.
—Attributed to Confucius

Ol' Blue Eyes Is Back.
—Frank Sinatra comes out of retirement after 16 months

Simon had been really looking forward to retirement. The constant pressure that came with his job had been getting to him. Too many meetings, too much travel, too much of everything.

Unfortunately, retirement didn't pan out quite like he'd hoped. Grocery shopping only gave him a limited sense of fulfilment and he found he missed the daily stream of emails and phone calls. He missed talking to his colleagues. He missed being in the middle of things. Basically, Simon felt lost.

I've come across a lot of Simons in my work. People who have enjoyed their career find it difficult to accept that it's over. They may recognize that they are entering a new stage in life, but they will probably have given little thought as to how they will deal with their changed status on an emotional level—and the demands their jobs placed on them may have left them with very little time to reflect. The result is that retirement comes as a serious let down.

Onboarding, also known as organizational socialization, refers to the process of integrating new employees into a company and providing them with the knowledge needed to become productive members. Like any relationship, long-term success in the employer-employee relationship requires clear management of expectations and building a shared vision for the future. Onboarding can have very positive results in the form of higher job satisfaction, better job performance, greater organizational commitment, and less likelihood of stress.

But what about "offboarding," or the process of helping people transition out of the organization after years of employment? Offboarding is particularly important when it is applied to the retirement process. Now we all live longer, retirement is different from what it used to be. Many people no longer envision an abrupt ending to their working life. Increasingly, many of us imagine the next step to be some kind of portfolio career in which we will take on a medley of part-time roles. At the same time, we also look forward to leaving behind the stresses and strains of full-time corporate life.

In fact, letting go can be very stressful. Having had intense discussions with many executives dealing with offboarding, I can testify that many experience this as a very challenging existential process. For many, the transition from work to retirement can be a rude awakening, particularly for men, for whom more their identity is often determined by their job. After having been in positions of power and control, many have difficulties letting go of their work friendships, business networks, and the fringe benefits and perks that came with the job. Most importantly, however, they must deal with the fact that work no longer provides the central structure of their life.

For many, offboarding can be an extremely uncomfortable, even frightening, transition. Like most major life-changing events—such as separation, divorce, birth, and death—retirement and letting go of a career also involve a painful emotional adjustment. While other life transitions have been the focus of decades of analysis and research, the emotional and psychological frontier of offboarding has remained relatively unexplored. So, what actions could we take to make letting go less stressful?

I suggest that the psychological process of letting go follows a similar pattern to the emotional phases that accompany other life transitions. Psychologists James Robertson and John Bowlby offer a useful template of the process—*protest*, *despair*, and *detachment*—based on how small children react to separation. The process lays out the pattern of how we begin to familiarize ourselves with the new landscape in which we find ourselves and how we orientate ourselves within it. As we might expect, some people sail through these stages while others experience difficulties or even get stuck.

For many who have enjoyed their career, offboarding involves an amount of grief. They find it difficult to accept that they can't carry on doing what they have been doing. Consciously, they recognize that they are entering a new stage in life, but they give little thought to how they will deal with their changed status on an emotional level. Often, the everyday demands of their job may leave them with very little time to do so. The reality is, that although they may have looked forward to this different stage in their life, when it arrives, it often is experienced as a serious let down. Some may get stuck at the stage of protest or despair, filled with disillusionment, abandonment, boredom, and feeling useless. A number may even experience having stress reactions and mental health issues. And it may sound dramatic but for some people retirement can even hasten death.

Offboarding requires major life adjustments. It isn't always easy to change a comprehensive work/life structure to some kind of retirement/life structure. To start with, take couples: making a successful transition may necessitate renegotiating domestic responsibilities and territorial disputes over cooking, shopping, household chores, and workspaces. This principally affects men who are no longer a breadwinner and live with a spouse or partner who hasn't offboarded. Depending on the cultural context, some men may experience their position at this stage in life as shameful or even parasitic. Furthermore, if their partner is working, the offboarder may find himself spending many hours at home alone. Unless he can find other meaningful activities (for example, grandparenting), this can contribute to feelings of insecurity, anxiety, and depression. Frankly, life can become lonely with no clear plan for the transition into retirement.

Offboarding necessitates reorientation, that is, building a new identity. Whether people have identified as a banker, an industrialist, a hospital director, or the president of a university, offboarding raises the question what they are now, when they no longer hold that position. In particular, people with high-skill careers may be left with feeling they are a nobody, and question their identity, purpose, and usefulness. They need to find answers to these questions to be able to continue living life meaningfully. From my observations when coaching senior executives, people going through the offboarding process fall into three types, which might be described as steadfast, experimenters, or disenchanted.

- *Steadfast* Some people, especially those with a specialized skill base, find ways to carry on what they have been doing. They may change organization, find some kind of part-time or interim position in their field of expertise, or take on an advisory role in the industry in which they have been working.
- *Experimenters* A smaller group of offboarders see retirement as a chance to do something very different. For them, the joy of reaching this stage of life is that it opens numerous opportunities. Those I have coached have gone on to do voluntary work, gone back to university to study topics they have always been interested in, and even started new ventures.

- *Disenchanted* Sadly, some offboarders remain stuck in the despair stage of the protest-despair-detachment cycle and do not know how to pick themselves up again. They may regret missed opportunities or feel that their life has been a failure. They run the risk of finding themselves in a long-lasting depressive phase, feeling disengaged from life. They miss the structure that their previous life offered—working to deadlines, finishing projects, or gaining promotion—and feel completely lost.

For a long time, offboarding was simply an exercise in financial planning. The psychological dimensions of retirement were not part of the human resource department's agenda. After all, before the turn of this century, we were not expected to live much beyond the traditional three-score years and ten. Now, given our much longer life span, assuring financial security is only one important element of the offboarding process. Proactive life planning—including the psychological effects of letting go—are now considered equally important. While each individual needs to take personal responsibility, HR professionals need to see offboarding as part of their portfolio.

What steps can you take to make offboarding less painful? From a *personal perspective*:

- Don't wait until the moment of letting go has arrived. While you are still actively working, start to diversify—expand your life beyond the workplace with voluntary work, recreational activities, hobbies, and membership of clubs and organizations that provide opportunities for building new activities and friendships. And keep on learning—enroll in practical or academic courses, for example.
- Maintain your relationships with friends and family members. The famous Harvard Longitudinal Study has shown that embracing community helps us to live longer and stay happy. Close relationships keep people happier throughout their life than money or fame.[1] Some executives are so focused on work that they ignore these important pillars of mental health.
- When you feel stuck, ask for help. A life/career coach or psychotherapist can assist you in identifying new avenues for growth. Most people will benefit from practicing self-reflection to learn who and what they are all about. Personal counselling, therapy and personal growth workshops can help us make these journeys into the self, to align values and behaviors in the next phase in life.

---

[1] https://www.theatlantic.com/magazine/archive/2013/05/thanks-mom/309287/.

From a *work* perspective:

- If you want to continue to use your skills but in a less active way, consider part-time or interim employment, or take on a board position. If you are an instinctively steadfast offboarder, this can be a smooth transitional process.
- Many executives I have met have found teaching an active outlet for their creative abilities. Generativity, concern for the future, the need to nurture and guide younger people and contribute to the next generation, can bring an enormous amount of satisfaction.
- If you feel the need for deeper connections with other people, try volunteering. Join voluntary organizations where your skillset can make an important contribution. Making time for voluntary work helps you make new friends, extend your network, and boost your social skills. Loneliness and isolation are two of the most serious social problems in the world today, and volunteering helps you make connections with other people and cultivate friendships with other volunteers.
- Mentor budding entrepreneurs or young executives. Many successful entrepreneurs have had mentors. Effective mentoring can have an inestimable value. As a mentor, you can provide reassurance, answer questions, and make suggestions that can help younger people navigate the business world. As networking is vital for company success, you can also use your connections to give a jumpstart to your mentees. You may even decide to be actively involved in their entrepreneurial ventures.

Companies shouldn't be passive bystanders in this process. Presently, too few of them play an active role in helping people transition, but this doesn't have to be the case. For example, I remember working with a very large premier strategic consulting firm that gave its senior partners a relatively early retirement date. However, helped by specially designed workshops and lengthy discussions with members of the organization's HR department, the outgoing partners were primed for the next phase in their life. In this organization, the offboarding process appeared to be as important as the process of onboarding.

Without preparing for offboarding, many people end up surprised at how difficult it is to transition to a new stage in life. The process may reactivate identity issues that occurred earlier in their life. People who give serious time and thought to what they will do after they let go of their present position experience a much smoother and more fulfilling transition. However, whatever new horizons offboarders pursue, it's important from a mental health perspective that their choices are anchored in meaning. As the writer Kahlil Gibran put it wisely, "To be able to look back upon one's life in satisfaction, is to live twice." For successful offboarders, retirement can provide a dual perspective from which to look back at their life and look forward to the next chapter.

Part III

Society

18

Is Democracy in the Workplace a Mirage?

> *A democracy is two wolves and one lamb voting on what to have for lunch.*
> —Benjamin Franklin
>
> *Democracy is the worst form of government, except for all the others.*
> —Winston Churchill

For many of us, democracy is the key principle of the governance of a nation state. Its core proposition is disarmingly simple: as members of a community, we should have an equal say in how life in that community is conducted. Democracy means that we are all equal before the law, that we can all have voice, and that we can contribute to the decision-making process (usually through means of a vote). And democracy is not a spectator sport; everyone is expected to participate in it. People are supposed to think for themselves. To make democracy work, however, institutional mechanisms need to be in place to guarantee that citizens have these options. Democracy means living in a society where information is shared. Naturally, freedom of the press will be essential to guarantee popular participation in the government's decisions and, similarly, there should be an independent judiciary. For a democracy to work, there need to be checks and balances against intimidation, harassment, violence, and corrupt practices. And let's not forget, the military should stay out of politics.

Interestingly, knowing the corrupting effects of power, it's surprising that most of those citizens who advocate democratic ideas work in organizations where they have very limited influence over their work—let alone over larger issues involving their leadership and organizational practices. Instead, most business organizations are controlled hierarchically by a small group of people at the top. Corporate democracy, in which all employees can have their say, is direly lacking. In most instances, the right to make decisions about an organization's policies remains the prerogative of the top executive team. Examples of true participative management in the business world are very hard to find. In the grand scheme of human events, democracy in organizational life tends to be the exception, not the rule.

One of the key characteristics of great organizations is that they give their people the opportunity to be heard and to have a degree of control over their destiny. Organizations that support these democratic principles provide a context that encourages people to give their best. When employees have a high degree of autonomy and are encouraged to be closely involved in decision-making processes, they experience greater job satisfaction. If this is the prevailing organizational modus operandi, people operate on a greater trust basis and there is less need for expensive command-and-control systems. In these instances, the interests of the group, as opposed to pure self-interest, prevail. We can presume that in these more democratically focused organizations, people are more engaged, loyal, creative, and productive.

However, as said, real democracy in the workplace tends to be rare and fleeting. In most instances, organizational power is concentrated at the top. Command-and-control systems are the norm. Consequently, many of the people who work in these organizations feel disengaged, helpless to appeal against what they perceive as misguided, uninformed, or poorly thought-out decisions. The latest Gallup poll figures of how employees experience organizational life, speak for themselves: employee engagement worldwide appears to be less than 30 percent.[1] Not surprisingly, the costs of corporate authoritarianism, in terms of organizational stress, high absenteeism, and reduced productivity, are substantial.

Given the general appreciation of democracy throughout society, and the lack of it in organizational life, the question is why are these kinds of organizations the rule, not the exception?

As more democratic decision-making processes can be unwieldy, an argument can be made that command-and-control systems make for greater simplicity. They enable speedier decision-making, and speed is a competitive advantage. Also, consensus-building isn't easy. Not only is it very time consuming, but it also contributes to conflict-avoidant behavior. As

---

[1] https://www.effectory.com/request/thankyou-download/?__FormGuid=64b7b54f-f264-4d70-b045-6001f999ee8c&__FormLanguage=en&__FormSubmissionId=11d4c502-7649-41ba-a855-d09fe0a071b7.

non-democratic decision-making practices are the rule, rather than the exception, it raises further questions: could it be that human beings are not genetically programmed for democratic living? Is autocracy a more natural state?

Taking an evolutionary perspective in considering these questions, we only have to look at our closest cousins, the chimpanzees. The archetypical organizational design for chimpanzees is hierarchical. Like human social behavior, the adult apes within each chimpanzee community engage in complex political maneuvers, involving scheming and physical intimidation, to move up the dominance hierarchy. The more successful ones often accomplish this by forming temporary alliances with a few other males to physically dominate the rest. These alliances are mainly formed for procreation, food-sharing, and mutual grooming. Interestingly, female chimpanzees are less involved in this constantly changing, often violent, political restructuring of their community.

In addition, male chimpanzee behavior has a darker side. Males occasionally murder members of other chimpanzee communities. Their motivation is not entirely clear. We could hypothesize that the net effect of these killings is to increase territory and food resources and reduce competition for potential mates. This kind of murderous behavior is also a characteristic of Homo sapiens.

Given the dominance fights we can observe among our closest relatives, we could conjecture that democracy is unnatural because it goes against our evolutionary programming, vital instincts, and impulses. At a very basic level—like the great apes—we are programmed to survive and reproduce. Again, like the great apes, we feel compelled to assert ourselves—relentlessly, unwittingly, and savagely—against those who stand in our way. We push other people aside, overstep them, overthrow them, even crushing them if necessary. Thus, behind the smiling façade of human civility, there persists the same blind drive toward self-assertion that we find in the animal realm—and constant striving to be top of the power pyramid. Could it be true that human nature appears to favor what we are desperately trying to avoid when we opt for democracy?

Moving from the evolutionary to the psychological perspective, we see that in turbulent situations, or in a state of high anxiety, human dependency reactions come to the fore. In these situations, we tend to regress. At the same time, we become attracted to "saviors," individuals we hope will guide us, and who can create the illusion of certainty in a highly uncertain world. In crisis situations, when we feel helpless, we are prepared to subjugate ourselves to autocratic leaders who appear to offer certainty. Thus, another explanation for why democracy is often so hard to find, could have something to do with our prevailing anxiety about living in a volatile world. It could very well be that democracy is not a natural state in that it will always hover in a delicate space between conflict and confusion. We have seen over and over again in human history that it doesn't take much for democracy to be tipped off-balance and self-destruct. Most often, however, the demise of democracy is a slow process of extinction due to apathy, indifference, and undernourishment.

We cannot draw much confidence about the strength of democracy from our own political history. As the philosopher Bertrand Russell put it, making a distinction between democracy and dictatorship, "Democracy; the fools have a right to vote; dictatorship; the fools have a right to rule." Most of the time, when we talk about democracy, we are referring to an ideal rather than an observable practice. But although we may never be able to reach true democracy, we shouldn't stop dreaming of it or trying to make it a reality. Democracy remains one of those elusive propositions whose promise, even if perpetually deferred, could be more important than its realization. Given the fact that democracy will always be a work in progress, we need to strive for "good enough" rather than perfection when building and maintaining democratic institutions.

Despite our evolutionary legacy and the fragility of true democracy, leaders should still strive to create best places to work where people believe that they have voice and that their opinions count. In other words, we should try to create authentizotic organizations, a term I devised by combining two Greek words: *authentikos* and *zootikos*. As a workplace label, *authentikos* implies an organization characterized by fair processes. This kind of workplace emphasizes self-actualization, which will contribute to a sense of effectiveness, competency, autonomy, and creativity in organizational members. The term *zootikos* means "vital to life." In an organizational context, it describes the way in which people are invigorated by their work and can find balance, commitment, and completeness, and where the need for exploration—closely associated with cognition and learning—is met.

Leaders of authentizotic organizations infuse their organizations with meaning. They effectively articulate what they want to accomplish by communicating a vision of what the organization stands for, highlighting its fundamental *raison d'être*, and recognizing each employee's contribution to its success. Subscribing to the credo "profit with purpose," they try to create a balance between what's good for the organization and what's good for the people who work there. They are not motivated by short-termism; they are in it for the long run. The authentizotic mindset relies on creating a culture of trust, mutual support, recognition, and engagement that unites people around a common vision—a people-centric culture where employees have meaningful work and give their best to the organization. In these organizations, people work in collaborative teams, feel secure, and are protected by safeguarding policies that put checks on the abuse of power. Therefore, in the summing up, the pursuit of the dream of greater organizational democracy can have a surprising outcome in the form of higher engagement, more successful and more humane places of work, and taking a macro perspective, a more livable world.

19

The Societal Costs of Loneliness

We are all so much together, but we are all dying of loneliness.
—*Albert Schweitzer*

Who knows what true loneliness is—not the conventional word but the naked terror? To the lonely themselves it wears a mask. The most miserable outcast hugs some memory or some illusion.
—*Joseph Conrad*

In the twenty-first century, the opening line of Harry Nilsson's song, "One is the loneliest number that you'll ever do," is truer than ever. Many of us experience loneliness no matter how many people we are with, and no matter how close we are to them. Loneliness is the most central and inevitable challenge of all human experiences. It is an elementary aspect of the human condition and an integral part of our journey through life. We are born alone and will die alone. Unfortunately, in a desperate effort to cope with loneliness, we fill our minds with noisy activities to drown out its silence.

In Chap. 8, I touched on the fact that the word loneliness pertains to the pain of being alone, while the word solitude can express the pleasure of being alone. Being alone is the physical state of being by ourselves, enjoying our own company. Being lonely means that something is missing. Loneliness is a psychological state of distress triggered by wanting to connect with someone but there being nobody to connect with. It refers to feelings of isolation and abandonment.

I would go so far as to suggest that solitude is necessary for us to thrive—even to feel more alive—but that isn't the case with loneliness. Many people look desperately for community to escape the fear of being alone and fail to discover that the ability to be solitary is a sign of mental health. Taking a psychological perspective, I see loneliness as indicative of poverty of the self, and the capacity for solitude as indicative of the richness of the self.

There have been many socially disruptive changes in contemporary society, including feelings of reduced organizational membership, increased working from home, unemployment, a surging senior population, greater detachment from nature, and less and less time to build meaningful relationships. More people than ever before live alone and feel lonely. Communities are no longer what they were. Today, it is just as easy to be lonely in a city as it is in the wilderness. Loneliness in a crowd is often the worst kind of loneliness. When we live in crowded places, it can be even harder to build relationships. In cities, it is easy to ignore others and easier for others to pay no attention to us. When there are fewer people around, it's more likely that people will take on responsibility, simply because they expect the gesture to be reciprocated. What worsens these feelings of being lonely in a crowd is that there are fewer and delayed marriages or partnerships in our society. Even among those who are together, many relationships seem to be strained, due to a lack of intimacy. Nothing is lonelier than being with someone and still feeling alone, to have someone physically present, but to feel there's no one in sight.

The loneliness equation is complicated by the fact that intergenerational solidarity is declining. The extended family is increasingly fractured and weakened. Social institutions like churches and neighborhood clubs have declined. Many people are no longer deeply embedded in their communities. Some futurists suggest that we have entered a dystopian age, living in a world that's dominated by technology, a contributing factor to feelings of disconnection and alienation. Social media have aggravated the problem. Often, when I look at Facebook or Instagram, it seems everyone else in the world is having a fabulous time and enjoying perfect relationships. Of course, I realize that this is not really the case. Smartphones, tablets, and computers, however, have turned into pseudo-defense systems to help us cope with loneliness. Our devices have become ideal crutches to lean on, especially when we feel anxious about filling the blank spaces in our day. Only on the Internet a person can be lonely and popular at the same time. Our compulsion to reach out to our phone every few minutes signifies our need to be needed by others—to seek attention while, at the same time, battling loneliness. The time we once spent on contemplation, "niksen," small talk or simply being bored, has now been filled by addiction to our screens.

Being connected to others in a meaningful way—not through screens—is a fundamental human need that is crucial to our well-being and survival. The pandemic, when our enforced two-dimensional life had us staring at screens for both work and entertainment, has made this need clearer than ever. Unfortunately, in our cyber age loneliness has become widespread and meaningful relationships are hard to find. For example, in the US, it is estimated that 25–45 percent of American adults report being chronically lonely. Although people of any age can be socially isolated, the risk of losing contact with friends, family, and community members becomes much greater as we age. In a study aiming to quantify the cost of loneliness in the US, it is estimated that among Americans aged 65 or older, social isolation costs the government nearly $7 billion in additional health care costs per year.[1] Sadly enough, the effects of loneliness on public health and the public purse are only anticipated to increase.

Loneliness, it seems, can lead to long-term fight-or-flight stress signaling, which will negatively affect our immune system. Loneliness can wreak havoc on our physical, mental, and cognitive health. The adverse health consequences of loneliness include depression, insomnia, and accelerated cognitive decline (increasing the risk of dementia), at every stage of life. In addition, lonely people are less likely to make and keep doctors' appointments, to take medicine, to exercise, and to eat a healthy diet. Most notably, social isolation and loneliness significantly increase the risk of premature mortality. It is estimated that they increase the odds of a premature death by 26 percent.[2]

Loneliness can accelerate during life transitions, such as the death of a loved one, a divorce, the empty nest, or a move to a new place. This kind of loneliness is reactive. More serious problems arise when loneliness becomes chronic. Chronic loneliness is most likely to set in when individuals lack the emotional, mental, or financial resources to satisfy their social needs or lack a social circle that can provide these benefits. In these situations, many of the negative health consequences of loneliness become more noticeable.

When loneliness becomes a preoccupation, it signifies that something must change and that it is high time to act. Awareness, however, is one thing, but taking action is a different matter. Too many people see loneliness as a shameful, embarrassing affliction that they have brought upon themselves in some obscure way. Consequently, they prefer to keep it hidden and not talk about it, while others, although realizing there is a problem, prefer not to react.

Finding solutions to chronic loneliness has proven to be challenging. It is not easy to develop effective interventions since there's no single underlying cause for loneliness. Different people are lonely for different reasons. There is

---

[1] https://qz.com/1439200/loneliness-costs-the-us-almost-7-billion-extra-each-year/.
[2] https://www.thecostofloneliness.org.

no one-size-fits-all kind of intervention. But if we plan to act, we must remember to address underlying causes. In many instances of chronic loneliness, we can identify childhood dynamics where neglect and abandonment were dominant themes. From the perspective of preventative maintenance, efforts to minimize loneliness should start at home, by helping children to understand that being alone does not mean loneliness. The challenge is to provide young people with the inner resources to combat loneliness. It also implies fostering environments in which children look out for and identify when their peers seem lonely or disconnected from others and will intervene.

Loneliness is a state of mind that comes to the fore when we lack the inner resources to manage our anxiety about feeling alone. Loneliness isn't always due to a lack of company; it can also be due to a lack of purpose. Having a purposeful life is a great antidote to loneliness. Unfortunately, as many of us have discovered, the worst place we can be is in our own head. Arguably, we would be less lonely if we accepted our own company. In other words, introversion can be a great strength. If we have a rich inner life, it is less likely that we will feel lonely. If that's the case, whatever challenges we face, we can draw on our inner resources. Loneliness does not necessarily come from having no people around but from being unable to communicate the things that are important to us—another issue a loneliness intervention needs to address.

There are many activities specifically designed to improve our social skills, ways of being that invite social support or increase opportunities for social interaction. For example, engaging people in community and social groups has positive mental health effects, reducing feelings of loneliness. We can all fight loneliness by engaging in random acts of kindness and altruistic activities. Sometimes, a seemingly simple thing, like discovering the comfort and support provided by a pet dog or cat, can be the answer.

A very effective action step to reduce loneliness—particularly for the elderly—is the creation of living communities. Joining a community can be a highly effective way to improve social connections. For example, today we can see a proliferation of co-housing communities and mixed-age residences, where residents share dining, laundry, and recreational spaces. The co-housing structure makes it easy to form clubs, organize child and elder care, carpools, and even celebrate events.

Psychotherapy can be very helpful in helping people overcome loneliness. Psychotherapists can address maladaptive social cognition and help people recognize and deal with their negative thoughts and self-perception and how they think others perceive them. They can also help lonely people unravel why the feeling of loneliness has become such an overriding concern. However, as

I know from experience, focusing inwards to address the negative thought processes underlying loneliness is not always an easy task.

Paradoxically, while recognizing that loneliness can be a serious health hazard, we shouldn't underestimate the value of solitude. There will be times when it can be very enriching to be alone. As many philosophers and psychologists have pointed out, personal growth and development often derive from solitude. Solitude gives us an opportunity to discover who we really are. It offers us the opportunity to dwell in our own mind, allowing us to think, and to imagine. Solitude may take us toward otherwise unreachable experiences of reality.

20

Bluebeard Revisited

Education is not the filling of a pail, but the lighting of a fire.
—William Butler Yeats

The cocks may crow, but it's the hen that lays the egg.
—Margaret Thatcher

While looking at disquieting news stories of women being abused and locked up by powerful men, I was reminded of the terrifying fairy tale *Bluebeard*. This French folktale, its most famous version written by Charles Perrault, was first published in 1697 in *Histoires ou contes du temps passé* (Stories or tales from past times). The tone of this bloodthirsty story is very different from the other stories in Perrault's collection, which included *Sleeping Beauty* and *Cinderella*. Here, there are no princes or princesses who live happily ever after. The tale of *Bluebeard* starts with a marriage between a wealthy man and a young woman, who, having left the safety of her home, subsequently witnesses a gruesome event. It is a story of deceit, death, murder, blood, and forbidden chambers, most likely inspired by the behavior of nobles who terrorized their people during the Middle Ages. Unfortunately, the theme of women being abused by their husbands tends to be universal. Since its publication, this particular story has never lost its fascination, and remains one of the most popular fairy tales. Its symbolic importance is reflected in the many versions to be found around the world, and it continues to serve as a template for numerous reinterpretations, in the theatre and the opera or on film.

Bluebeard is the story about a murderous husband (Bluebeard) and a locked chamber filled with the bodies of his previous wives. Bluebeard, although notorious for his ugly appearance, uses his wealth to tempt women into marriage, after which they are never seen again. After each wedding, he presents his new wife with all the house keys and tells her she can enter every room—except one.

Of course, this prohibition is an invitation to do precisely the opposite. As we expect, Bluebeard's new wife—like all those before her—yields to her curiosity, unlocks the forbidden room, and discovers a grisly scene: the floor of the room is covered with blood and the bodies of many women are hanging from the walls. Faced with this dreadful sight, she panics, and drops the key on the bloody floor. She tries desperately to wash the blood from the key, but it is enchanted and can't be cleaned. When Bluebeard returns, he finds the blood on the key and declares that the consequence of her defiance is to suffer the same fate as the other wives. But his new wife has no intention of joining the corpses in the forbidden chamber. She begs for a little time to pray before her death and manages to summon help from her sister and brothers, who arrive at the castle in time to slay Bluebeard and save her life.

The fairy tale has a happy ending, for the latest wife at least. On Bluebeard's death, she becomes mistress of his castle and estate. She remarries but this time on her own terms. Powerless, dependent, and abused as Bluebeard's wife, she is transformed into someone who is in control, a person in her own right.

One perennial message contained in the Bluebeard story is the danger implicit in male-female relationships. In addition, the story of Bluebeard is often interpreted as a cautionary tale about curiosity, a moralizing note that women should obey their husbands' wishes if they don't want to come to harm. This message fitted perfectly with the view held by Perrault's seventeenth-century contemporaries: knowledgeable, powerful, and willful women were perceived as dangerous—a message that still holds sway today.

However, fairy tales shouldn't be taken literally. They often turn out to be a dance between several unconscious archetypical forces—in the case of Bluebeard, masculine and feminine—that manifest themselves in the collective and the individual psyche.

The tale of Bluebeard taps into deep undercurrents of sex and violence. For example, taking a rather simplistic psychoanalytic perspective, many sexual associations can be made with the key, the lock, and the forbidden chamber with its hidden contents. The key could be associated with the phallus, the keyhole with the vagina, and the room with the womb. The bloody key could suggest a woman's loss of virginity.

In truth, there are ways to interpret the Bluebeard story. From whatever angle it is looked at, it remains a very troubling tale because of its timelessness. Many women have lived and continue to live this story. Naively, they begin a relationship, to discover that their chosen partner turns out to be a monster; and that they are trapped in emotional and/or physical abuse. Every day, we hear stories and testimonials about the abuse of women.

A fascinating part of the tale is that the wife disobeys Bluebeard's order and opens the door to the forbidden room. The obvious question is, if Bluebeard doesn't want his wives to go into that room, why does he give them the key? And the obvious answer is that he expects them to disobey his orders and give him an excuse to murder them. The biblical story of Adam and Eve is a prime example of this kind of trap. Given a prohibition, Eve's curiosity is piqued; she gives in to temptation and eats the forbidden fruit. Her defiance comes at a high price, and man's fall from grace is attributed to her desire for knowledge.

Conversely, we could look at curiosity and defiance as symbolizing life and transformation for the wife, and death for Bluebeard. When she disobeys her husband and opens the locked door, the wife loses her innocence, but she acquires volition and knowledge. She becomes conscious of the ugly reality of male-female power dynamics but, at the same time, she has created an opening for truth and inner transformation.

In fact, the wife's curiosity—coupled with her defiance and astuteness in navigating the consequence of her actions—could be a life saver. Without it, she would never have freed herself from the constraints of the marital relationship. In other words, a more appropriate interpretation of the Bluebeard tale is to see it as a story of a woman becoming independent. Thus, contrary to what Perrault suggested, women's natural curiosity should not be stifled. Through curiosity, the wife discovers what lies beyond the appearance of things. She attains knowledge, becomes more conscious and develops a sense of purpose.

This fairy tale also makes quite clear that men feel threatened by curious and daring women. Many seem afraid to share knowledge with women and prefer to keep them dependent and disempowered. And sadly enough, there are still far too many Bluebeards among us who think this way. Many men still hang on to the idea that women are inferior and should be kept down. The roots of this prejudice lie deep in our evolutionary history. Despite promising progress in some areas, discrimination against women continues to persist worldwide.

Clearly, for the Bluebeards among us, knowledge means power. This explains why many men prefer their women to remain uneducated. Far too many men fear empowering women. By ordering his wife not to open the locked room, Bluebeard wants to keep her ignorant and dependent. In that respect, he is representative of many manipulative men who play mind games to entrap women emotionally and physically.

As of today, there are still millions of women who have no control over their own life and body and there is no place in the world where women live free from violence. Laws explicitly mandating "wifely obedience" still govern marital relations in far too many countries. The belief that women must be subjugated to the wishes of men is far too common. This attitude has excused slavery, violence, forced prostitution, genital mutilation and national laws that do not consider rape as a serious crime. The laws in far too many countries also continue to institutionalize second-class status for women regarding nationality and citizenship, health, education, and marital, employment, parental, inheritance, and property rights. In many countries women are still barred from participating fully in social and economic life. And most of the world's poorest people are women and girls.

Although women in most countries have now the right to education, equal access to education remains a problem. Yet education is the key for women to achieve economic independence. Unfortunately, many men fail to understand that educated women have healthier, better educated children and these children are going to be the building blocks for a better society. Our challenge, if we want to create a more equitable world, is to get rid of the Bluebeards in society who block women's access to education. If we want to change the world, we must accept that educating women is the most powerful weapon in our arsenal. We should heed the well-known African saying, "If you educate a man, you educate an individual. But if you educate a woman, you educate a nation."

21

Do We Get the Leaders We Deserve?

The lion is most handsome when looking for food.
—Rumi

A narcissist will deliberately damage other people in pursuit of their own selfish desires but may regret and will in some circumstances show remorse for doing so, while a malignant narcissist will harm others and enjoy doing so, showing little empathy or regret for the damage they have caused.
—John Garner

Do we get the leaders we deserve? I hope not, but sometimes I wonder. The coronavirus pandemic has been the most serious crisis we have experienced since World War II. As things stand, we need competent leaders more than ever. But looking at the present leadership landscape worldwide is not exactly encouraging. In too many instances, there is a lack of trust. Even though the virus created a global pandemic, too many countries have reacted selfishly. As one after another they started to circle the wagons, questions were raised about the future of global collaboration and a return to the nation state.

Dictators and semi-dictators galore have been elected by appealing to the lowest common denominator. Some of them have even created cult-like environments, getting a segment of the population to follow them like lemmings. By catering to people's "wish to believe"—promising them miracles—we have seen many leaders who can be best described as malignant narcissists come to power. Is this really the kind of leader we want to guide us through crises?

What is meant by a malignant narcissist? Let me tell you. First, it is not the kind of person you'd like to meet in a dark alley. All narcissistic personality disorders are problematic, but malignant narcissism is by far the most disturbing and damaging. As the psychoanalyst and philosopher Erich Fromm (who invented the diagnosis of malignant narcissism) noted, this kind of personality "lies on the borderline between sanity and insanity."[1] Malignant narcissists combine the characteristics of narcissistic and anti-social (psychopathic) personality disorder. So, apart from being prime narcissists—that is, totally egocentric—they also possess a darker, ruthless side.

Often malignant narcissists believe that the world should revolve around them. They exaggerate their talents or achievements. But notwithstanding their feelings of superiority, they also need their daily dose of flattery. They like (and need) to be told that they are the greatest. And the people around them, knowing what's good for them, quickly realize that flattery is the prescription for career success. They are obsequious, knowing that if they don't give the malignant narcissist a daily "fix," they will not last very long. However, malignant narcissists, for all their boasting and bragging, are deep down extremely insecure. They have a very fragile ego, which is why they need constant external validation.

To all this, we can add a sense of entitlement, the dark influence of envy, a tendency to devaluate others, little or no empathy for other people's emotions or feelings, and the constant need to take advantage of others. Malignant narcissists pursue their self-interests with no moral restrictions and total disregard for other people's feelings. They don't care who they hurt as long as they get their way.

Furthermore, malignant narcissists see the world in black-and-white terms. People are either for them or against them. There is no middle ground. They are masters of polarization with a weakness for crazy conspiracy theories and a false sense of victimization. They will demonize the press, minorities, indeed anyone who opposes them.

The possibility of being wrong is a reality no malignant narcissist will face. Even the slightest criticism will provoke extreme defensive reactions. In response to anger, embarrassment, or any other emotion, the malignant narcissist becomes highly aggressive. When irritated or angry, they enjoy humiliating others, especially in public situations. They like bullying people.

If there is evidence of error or wrongdoing on their part, a malignant narcissist will insist that the facts and evidence are wrong. Agreements are treated as nothing more than the beginning of a discussion; their idea of honoring them is very fluid. According to their mindset, only weaklings take such conciliatory approaches. They have a gift for playing people off against each other

---

[1] Erich Fromm (1964). *The Heart of Man: Its Genius for Good and Evil.* New York: Harper & Row.

and are keenly perceptive of their adversaries' Achilles heels. They are truly Machiavellian. However, malignant narcissists can also have a charming exterior. If it is to their own advantage, they will tell others what they want to hear, using exaggeration and embellishment to impress them.

Unfortunately, as we see all too often, malignant personalities seek out leadership positions. They are very effective in appealing to the lowest level of human sentiment and taking advantage of group regression. They are adept at externalizing their own needs and making them look like the needs of society. As they surround themselves with sycophants, the little judgment they possess becomes further impaired by this behavior pattern. Unsurprisingly, their inability to tolerate criticism prevents malignant narcissists from ever receiving or hearing constructive feedback, aggravating their lack of judgment, and encouraging mediocre or even disastrous decisions.

Despite their known fallacies, these leaders still manage to attract followers: the lure of power, glory, and money overwhelms any call to conscience. Too many of the people who work for them are in pursuit of position over principle. But while they are attracted to these leaders because they provide them with a power base, they can easily make a false step and fall out of the leader's favor at any moment.

Within an organization, this type of leader creates a toxic, paranoid, and even depressive work environment. Unsurprisingly, the most competent people will not be attracted to such a place and, even if they choose to work there, will not last long. They will be fired or leave of their own volition. Thus, in the malignant narcissist's entourage, creative, productive people are very hard to find—a serious drawback, especially in the current, unprecedented conditions created by the coronavirus and the measures needed to contain it.

The leaders we need now must have the ability to look at things systemically. They need to understand interrelationships and long-term development. Effective leaders rely on a capability for reflection and emotional intelligence and need a solid sense of self-worth to be able to withstand the pressures that come with the job. This kind of leader also needs a strong ethical compass to steer clear of the corrupting influences that can come with the job. Unfortunately, many of the world's leaders lack all of the above, as well as moral authority and trust.

It is downright dangerous to have malignantly narcissistic leaders in charge, not just for an individual country, but for the entire world. Leaders who are obsessed with alternative facts, conspiracy theories, racism, denial of science, and delegitimization of the press can't be trusted to do the right thing. And with the world in great turmoil, trust in the political system is something we need now more than ever.

22

Why Do Societies Regress?

> *The first human who hurled an insult instead of a stone was the founder of civilization.*
> —Sigmund Freud
>
> *History proves that all dictatorships, all authoritarian forms of government are transient. Only democratic systems are not transient. Whatever the shortcomings, mankind has not devised anything superior.*
> —Vladimir Putin

As a student of leadership, when I look at the state of the world, particularly at political leadership, I don't get a warm feeling. In Turkey, President Recep Tayyip Erdoğan locks up journalists who disagree with him. In the Philippines, Rodrigo Duterte's claim to fame is to shoot to kill alleged drug pushers. In Brazil, Jair Bolsonaro is infamous for his indifference toward the destruction of the Amazonian rain forest. In India, Narendra Modi, demonizes Muslims. In Saudi Arabia, Prince Mohammed Bin Salman has been heavily implicated in the murder of a journalist, Jamal Khashoggi. In Hungary, Viktor Orbán happily violates European regulations and the rule of law. In Russia, Vladimir Putin, a master puppeteer, has supported the genocidal regime of Syria's Bashar al-Assad, and overseen illegal operations in other countries. High on this depressing hit parade is US ex-president Donald Trump, who tried his hardest to transform the US into a kind of banana republic, inspiring many other authoritarian regimes in the process. A country whose values once made it a role model for other countries now has a lot of ground to make up. Many nations that once looked up to the US, struggle to account for his popularity, given his undemocratic practices, including an attempt to incite his followers to engage in a coup.

No wonder that societies regress. When they do, dysfunctional leadership and disturbing group behavior come to the fore, the one encouraging the other. To make sense of what's going on, however, psychology has come to the rescue.

When there is great uncertainty in any society—national, regional, organizational—particularly the collapse of traditional social structures, a threat to cultural identity, or economic crises, the conditions are created for large group regression. In these situations, people rapidly fall into dependency patterns, and look for a strong leader who will provide them with the guidance and reassurance needed to deal with their existential security. They will be vulnerable to the siren songs of would-be leaders who seem to understand their predicament, claim to have all the solutions, and provide a sense of security. When groups experience an existential crisis, they will unite behind this type of leader, assuming that all their problems will be solved in some magical way. The imagined "savior" will give them "voice," reaffirm their communality, provide them with a common ideology, and protect them from external threats. These leaders depict a simple world consisting of friend and enemies, a division between "us" versus "them." Soon, the members of the group, given their dependency reactions, encouraged by their leader, develop a shared sense what's good and what's bad—a very absolute morality. Whatever their new group identity becomes, it must be protected against people that oppose it.

Given these regressive processes, the group's capacity for independent thinking and decision-making will be reduced. Being part of this "special" group provides a sense of belonging and power, a process of identification with the leader on whom they project all their powerful fantasies. As the idealized (and feared) "savior," the leader will take care of them all, lead the way, and them where to go. The followers no longer need to take responsibility. The leader becomes their consciousness, freeing them from any moral constraints. While idealizing the person in charge, all their aggression is directed to the out-groups. As this regression continues, there will be a loss of personal identity and reduced capacity for independent thinking. People who try to retain their personal identity and independent judgment will be expelled.

People with paranoid and narcissistic characteristics tend to emerge in situations of societal regression, and those with malignant narcissistic tendencies are ideally placed to assume leadership positions. They are characterized by inordinate self-centeredness, a sense of superiority, lack of empathy, exploitative behavior, the constant need for external stimulation, paranoia, vindictiveness, underdeveloped ethical values, and general anti-social behavior patterns. Despite all this, they may function highly effectively in regressive group situations, where they are able to satisfy the basic needs of regressed group members.

Unfortunately, under this kind of leadership critical thinking will evaporate. As the cognitive capacities of the leader's followers are reduced, the followers will easily be seduced by simplistic slogans—black-and-white thinking—that replace systemic, complex analysis. Leaders' aggressive, even dehumanizing, behavior toward people who don't accept their binary view of the world, will be welcomed and seen as a courageous, heroic stand. Their activities will be celebrated. Leader-follower interactions will become cult-like. The leader's evident dishonesty will be rationalized and morally justified. People who show any sign of independent thinking will be cast out, ridiculed and demeaned. Any sign of disloyalty will be severely punished.

Clearly, there is a need for independent social structures to act as a counterweight to the behavior of such leaders. If there are no countervailing powers, leaders can go too far. An independent judiciary, a free press, and other independent institutions will prevent such developments. Strong institutions can limit the damage caused by regressive processes. There need to be checks and balances—a separation of power to make leaders accountable. Lord Acton's famous statement that "power tends to corrupt, and absolute power corrupts absolutely," should always be kept in mind.

23

Drinking the Kool-Aid

About 50 percent of politics is definitely obnoxious in as much as it poisons the utterly incompetent mind of the masses. We are on our guard against contagious diseases of the body, but we are exasperatingly careless when it comes to the even more dangerous collective diseases of the mind.
—Carl Jung

I have often noticed how primate groups in their entirety enter a similar mood. All of a sudden, all of them are playful, hopping around. Or all of them are grumpy. Or all of them are sleepy and settle down. In such cases, the mood contagion serves the function of synchronizing activities.
—Frans de Waal

Recently, I was looking at a painting by Bruegel the Younger, sometimes called "The Dance of St. John or St. Vitus." It portrays a strange social phenomenon that took place in Europe between the fourteenth and seventeenth centuries, a dancing "plague," a curse St. Vitus supposedly put on people leading a sinful life. His curse made people behave very bizarrely. In a kind of trance state, they felt compelled to dance. This strange phenomenon is one of the earliest-recorded cases of a psychic epidemic or a mass hysterical reaction.

Chronicles record how thousands of people would dance, screaming in agony about terrible visions. In a state of delirium, they would implore priests and monks to save their soul. They would *dance for hours* and by the time the frenzy ended, many of the dancers had died from cardiac arrest, stroke, or sheer exhaustion.

A contributing factor to this strange phenomenon was a deeply rooted popular belief that angry spirits could inflict a dancing plague. As many victims of this dancing mania could have been psychologically unstable, they must have been highly impressionable. According to historical records, the dancing plague would recur every so often, when physical and mental distress rendered people more than usually suggestible.

The longevity and reach of St. Vitus' dance illustrate the power of suggestibility. However, several preconditions needed to be in place for it to become so widespread. It didn't just emerge from thin air. Mass hysteria thrives on mystery, secrecy, and suspicion and needs a catalyst for such dramatic social contagion. This mass psychogenic illness was preceded by significant psychological distress throughout Europe, caused by famine, economic depression, and widespread death. Rising anxiety, combined with the power of suggestion, was easily converted into mass hysteria.

These psychic epidemics aren't just quaint historical phenomena. Similar strange incidents have continued to occur. Our history is full of examples of distorted beliefs rendering disastrous social consequences. We only have to think of the Crusades, witch hunts, tulip mania, moral panics involving alleged satanic abuse against children, and so on. History is littered with the scarred remnants of forms of groupthink.

Mass hysteria or psychogenic illness produces a constellation of symptoms often suggestive of an organic illness but with no organic cause. It demonstrates how large groups of people can easily be convinced of things with no basis of hard evidence. As social animals, human beings often act in ways that defy logic or reason. In fact, we can consider these mass hysterical outbursts as a feature of human evolution. Our Paleolithic ancestors could have endowed us with the cognitive and emotive architecture that make us attuned to environmental threats. To be more precise, when faced with danger, we don't take our time to contemplate and weigh the evidence. Far from it—we appear to be programmed to feed off each other's emotions. When faced with danger, our reflective thinking is easily subverted by groupthink. Unfortunately, this easily leads to panic reactions.

From a neurological point of view, fear seems to disconnect our neocortex, the center for higher brain functions such as motor commands, sensory perception, conscious thought, and spatial reasoning. When this happens, reflectivity goes out of the window. In these situations, we apply a "fight or flight" survival response to danger. By behaving in this manner, we create an ideal breeding ground for emotional contagion, leading to mass hysterical reactions.

When we are in the thrall of a psychotic reaction, several psychodynamic variables are at work, including impaired reality testing, primitive defensive mechanisms, and a fragile sense of identity. First, people caught up in a psychotic episode are delusional. Consequently, confused and disordered thought processes or emotions, wildly inconsistent with external reality, come to the fore. Second, people resort to primitive defensive reactions, such as splitting ("us" versus "them") and projection (projecting our own unacceptable qualities or feelings onto others). Third, people become confused about who they are and how they feel about themselves.

Interestingly, many members of the "cult of Trump" showed these behavior patterns. For example, there is their inability to accept the reality of the result of the 2020 presidential election, when Trump lost the possibility of a second term to his opponent Joe Biden. Their popular slogan, "Stop the steal," would be illustrative of their confused thought processes. Or take the fact that—despite hundreds of thousands of deaths—that many continued to believe that the coronavirus pandemic was a hoax. Again, we could observe their use of primitive defense mechanisms in the way that they see the world as "us" versus "them." They perceived a world full of conspiracies. Furthermore, many seemed to feel they have lost out in the lottery of life. A considerable number (particularly uneducated white males) believed—a conviction that carried a degree of truth—that they have been deprived of status and power. Being a member of the Trump cult helped them to shore up a very shaky identity.

Apart from experiencing psychotic-like behavior patterns, these people also seemed to be the victims of groupthink. Groupthink occurs when the desire for harmony in a decision-making group overrides a realistic, fact-driven appraisal of the alternatives. A group of well-intentioned people will make irrational or non-optimal decisions spurred on by the urge to conform or because they believe that dissent is impossible. In these situations, groups will rapidly form opinions that match the group's consensus rather than critically evaluate all the information. Unsurprisingly, groups in which dissent is discouraged or openly punished are more likely to engage in groupthink when making decisions, ignoring ethical or moral implications.

Groupthink is most likely to occur when groups feel threatened, either physically or in terms of their identity, or when a highly persuasive leader encourages members of the group to agree with his or her opinion. These are typically leaders who create a psychotic, alternative reality driven by anxiety and social media, which have proven highly effective in creating a virtual fantasy world. Unsurprisingly, extreme forms of groupthink and mass psychogenic illness are closely intertwined.

For example, the attempted coup at the US Capitol in January 2021 has been a recent example of how groupthink can contribute to the creation of a psychotic situation that escalated into a form of mass hysteria. It has illustrated how easily a collective state of mind can be created, and how easily large groups of people can be convinced of something that has no basis in evidence or logic. It's extremely frightening that tens of millions of people still believe former President Trump's "truth" that Joe Biden lost the election and became president through fraud. It indicates what a mega disinformation center like Trump can accomplish. It demonstrates clearly how mass hysteria will trump evidence.

In fact, rather than raising our eyebrows or being amused by it, we should regard the dancing plague of the Middle Ages as a warning against the harmful effects of social contagion, especially as, in our day-and-age, the danger of social contagion has been magnified immeasurably by the reach of the Internet and social media. The lack of critical reasoning, fed by obsessive news coverage (fake or otherwise), and enabled by demagogue-like leaders, has created very fertile conditions for groupthink. It has led to the formation of global groups that share delusional thoughts on a scale seldom witnessed in human history.

Today, it is far too easy to create cult-like mindsets, where all issues are painted as a struggle between good and evil, black and white, rooted in the biases of a chosen cult. Cult-like behavior has become more systemic and widespread than ever before. Huge numbers of people are willing "to drink the Kool-Aid," in other words, ready to accept distorted ideas due to popularity, peer pressure, or persuasion.

Distorting reality is hardly a new political tool. The willingness to be deceived has always been a driving force in politics. Many populist leaders have been able to conjure their followers into believing practically anything, realizing that, given their position of authority, their words take on the aura of truth. However, they may be unaware that they are setting psychotic-like processes in motion. In countries like Hungary, Poland, Turkey, and the Philippines, all governed by populist leaders, the distortion of truth seems to be par for the course. Even the UK's premier, Boris Johnson, is a skillful practitioner in creating alternative realities. All these leaders should remember the old saying that "he who rides a tiger is afraid to dismount." Unfortunately, as they take others on this wild ride, many innocent people also risk being devoured.

Nearly a century ago, the utility of cult-like behavior on a grand scale was first exploited by leaders like Adolf Hitler, Josef Stalin, and Mao Zedong. Mental contagion flourished under their regimes. We can all see the legacy these demagogues left the world and, given that awareness, it is imperative that the tendency toward cult-like behavior is broken.

Fortunately, a psychotic break with reality does not necessarily mean societies or individuals will share Humpty-Dumpty's fate. People do get put back together again, but it can be an uphill struggle. It's difficult to eliminate groupthink and cult-like behavior and make people face reality—particularly difficult in the world in which we live today. We have plenty to be anxious about. We are dealing with the growing reality of global warming, the ever-present possibility of nuclear disaster, increasing income inequality, terrorist threats, and, of course, a persistent global pandemic. Times of great uncertainty like ours are natural breeding grounds for mental contagion and mass hysterical reactions.

During mass hysteria, the human mind goes on the hunt for information that fits the narrative that helps explain the extant anxiety. And in a world of factoids, seeded by social media as the new "weapon of mass destruction," it isn't difficult to find a wide range of explanations. How do we know which are correct? Social media will quickly lead us down a rabbit hole littered with untruths. It is very hard to weed out all the available subjectiveness to find objective, accurate information to help reduce our level of anxiety. Yet doing nothing isn't the answer; something must be done. In this context, it is interesting to read what a major editorial writer of *The New York Times* has to say:

> Folks, we just survived something really crazy awful: four years of a president without shame, backed by a party without spine, amplified by a network without integrity, each pumping out conspiracy theories without truth, brought directly to our brains by social networks without ethics—all heated up by a pandemic without mercy.[1]

Thomas Friedman's comments highlight that something needs to be done to prevent this from happening again. Various macro and micro steps need to be taken to manage another flood of misinformation.

From a macro perspective, the actions of public institutions and the media are pivotal in the management of mass hysterical reactions. But to fight emerging paranoia, the collaboration of various public bodies is needed, capable of performing a range of preventative measures. Governments have an important role to play to counter misinformation with hard facts. They have the responsibility to focus on facts and debunk fiction. If not, as we have seen repeatedly, conspiracy theories can infect the real world with lethal effects.

In creating a fact-based dialogue, governmental leaders need to emphasize the importance of experts, while accepting that there could be a spectrum of

---

[1] https://www.nytimes.com/2021/01/19/opinion/trump-presidency.html?referringSource=articleShare.

expert opinions. Simply dismissing the views of experts—as we have all seen being done, particularly in the context of the pandemic—will erode the foundations of a well-functioning, fact-based society. The presence of devil's advocates, people who will help prevent the emergence of groupthink, is only to be recommended. After all, when everybody thinks alike, there's a good chance that nobody is thinking.

While keeping in mind the preeminence of free speech, there will be situations when governments may well decide that conspiracy theories have become so harmful that they need to be suppressed. Leaving these decisions to the leaders of social media companies is highly questionable. The leaders of the tech giants, with their eye on shareholder value, are not the right people to make these decisions about ethical behavior. Some kind of oversight body is needed. When necessary, governments could be required to put sanctions on those who profit from harmful irrationality.

Of course, in the case of politicians who peddle and exploit conspiracy theories, there is an old-fashioned way of dealing with them, which is to vote them out of office. Given the demagoguery that abounds, however, they are not always so easy to stop.

Educational institutions also have an important role to play. Given the important role social media play in education, they should make strenuous efforts to help students discriminate fact from fiction. Prevention is always better than attempting remedial action after the fact.

From a micro perspective, we should never allow other people to think and make decisions for us. We should learn to think for ourselves, as an antidote to psychic contagion. If we cannot think for ourselves, we no longer own our own lives.

From this perspective, skepticism can be a virtue. What governmental or other leaders say should never be taken at face value. We need look no further back than Trump's years in the White House, or the campaign for Britain to leave the European Union, to see how dangerous deliberate disinformation can be. We have to acknowledge that governments and corporations are capable of conspiring to do bad things. To paraphrase Rudyard Kipling, "If we can keep our head when all about us are losing theirs," we will nurture our reflective side and protect our mental health. If we don't, mass hysteria will overwhelm logic, values, and the rule of law, and a livable, sane society will fall by the wayside.

Epilogue

Those who can make you believe absurdities, can make you commit atrocities.
—*Voltaire*
The more often a stupidity is repeated, the more it gets the appearance of wisdom.
—*Voltaire*

As I end this book of essays on the human condition, I'm reminded of Voltaire's novella *Candide*. When I first read it, I was enraptured with this outrageous tragicomedy. The many dreadful events that the protagonists experience made me laugh and cry. Not surprisingly, immediately after its publication, *Candide* was widely banned, which only increased the book's popularity. Eventually, it became recognized as one of the great achievements of Western literature. Now, more than 250 years after its initial publication, the novella hasn't lost its relevance.

In *Candide*, Voltaire parodies many clichés of adventure and romance but caricatures them in a very much matter of fact tone. However, given its surrealistic content, the novella is not only a satire but also an extremely subversive work. Reading it, we follow the main characters as they travel the world, experiencing horror after horror, but taking all these events in their imperturbable stride. While the horrors described—flogging, rape, robbery, unjust execution, disease, earthquake, betrayal, and crushing ennui—point to the cruelty and folly of humanity, the protagonists behave as if Teflon-coated: nothing dents their optimistic attitude. They are like the actors in a Monty

Python movie, acting out situations that are genuinely dreadful, but nevertheless amusing due to their absurdity. With its extreme use of satire, *Candide* gave Voltaire an opportunity to ridicule religion, theologians, governments, armies, philosophies, and philosophers, all hidden under a thin veil of naïveté.

At the danger of oversimplifying, in *Candide* we are presented with the story of a gentle man who, though pummeled and slapped in every direction by fate, clings desperately to the belief that he lives in "the best of all possible worlds." While taking a trip around the world, during which he is exposed to innumerable dreadful events, he discovers—contrary to the teachings of his distinguished tutor, Pangloss—that everything is not always for the best. The novel shows Candide's gradual, but painful disillusionment as he witnesses and experiences one hardship after the other. It makes him realize that he doesn't live in "the best of all possible worlds."

Initially, we may be fooled by deeming the novella a witty, bantering tale. In reality, however, it was no fable. For Voltaire, it was reportage about the current state of his world, set deliberately among the headlines of the day. In fact, *Candide* is actually a tale of moral outrage about what was happening at the time it was written. Against a background of the horrors of human cruelty, Voltaire ends his novella with the words, "*Il faut cultiver notre jardin*"—"We must cultivate our garden." And this strange ending has retained its enigmatic quality. It could very well be that *Candide* is really Voltaire's Garden. As a "gardener," he plants ironies and contradictions in the hope that they can eventually bloom and inspire a solution—that in cultivating our own garden, we might find the answers to save a miserable world, answers that he was unable to find. Clearly, Voltaire's *Candide* is social criticism at its best. The novella enabled him to expose the failings of his society: to critique political and religious oppression, sexual violence against women, and the corrupting power of money. No wonder that his protagonist never can find true happiness.

Voltaire's ultimate message is that idle talk solves nothing. Philosophizing about life isn't good enough. As human beings we need to take action to create a better world. And to enable this to happen, we should start with ourselves ("cultivate our garden"). Even though, at times, matters may seem hopeless, we have some control what we can do as individuals.

Many of the themes that the novella touches on retain their relevance today. All of us come into the world as naïve as Candide, to become gradually disenchanted as we experience the realities of life. All too often, our desire to live in a caring environment where we can find order, clarity, and rationality is disrupted by a world of increasing change, where the future is less and less predictable. But although all often seems lost—as the story of *Candide* seems to suggest—we shouldn't give up hope. As Voltaire points out, the world can be made better by human effort. But if we want to live in a more livable world, it will require action by all of us.

The terrible pandemic that we have experienced since late 2019 has illustrated this need for action more than ever. It makes us realize that in life, the unimaginable—like the tragic ending of Aeschylus that I describe in the Foreword of this book—is always possible. But even though life can spring these surprises on us, we should not remain passive bystanders and accept what fate seems to offer. Fate will play its cards but just because it doesn't seem to have dealt us the right ones, we shouldn't give up. On the contrary, we should make the best out of the cards we have been dealt. Once we realize the extraordinary power we have to construct our life, we'll be able to move from passive bystanders to co-creators of our own fate.

When faced with world problems such as war, hunger, overpopulation, nuclear weapons, terrorism, and global warming, it is easy to become overwhelmed by feelings of helplessness. Yet we aren't helpless. We do have some control over our life. As the Dalai Lama said, "With realization of one's own potential and self-confidence in one's ability, one can build a better world." As I have tried to show in the various essays in this book, by "cultivating our garden" we should be able to deal with the suffering and misfortunes that surround us. If we try, we all have it in us to make this world a better place.

Of course, we may have to start with small steps, one day at a time. But these small steps will add up. And in taking them, we will not be alone. Instigating change isn't for the selected few. We can all contribute, however small. Far too often we look for the big things and forget that it is the small things that really matter. Just imagine what could happen if billions of people made the sort of small changes that help make the world a better place. Just imagine how powerful the accumulative effect could be.

Substantial change comes about when people are enabled to use their thinking and their energy in a new way, using different systems of thought, different language, and having fresh visions of the future. It's here that education plays an important role. If we want to create more balanced individuals, more effective leaders, more humane organizations, and more equitable societies, our main challenge is to provide our children with the kind of education that provides the foundation for this to happen.

But building a better world will not be possible unless we all, individually, become more self-conscious. The Ancient Greek aphorism, "Know thyself," is as relevant today as it has always been. To that end each of us must work for his or her own improvement, and at the same time accept our share in a general responsibility for all humanity. Building a better "I" will be the first step toward building a better world.

As individuals, we can organize socially, politically, and economically, and we can organize according to our values. As a people, we aren't helpless. That being the case, and given the fragile state of our planet, our generation has the responsibility to make our ever-more connected world a more hopeful, stable, and peaceful place. To make this happen, we need to be accountable to the next generation and bequeath to them a world that inspires them in which they want to live. It is our responsibility to leave the world in a better shape than we found it. We should remind ourselves that dreams are important but that dreaming alone doesn't make them come true. Action is what makes things happen. Hard work creates change. In the words of Nelson Mandela, "It is in our hands to make the world a better place."

Index

A

Abandonment, 93, 105, 108
Absenteeism, 70, 100
Accountability, 84, 85, 88
Acton, John Dalberg-Acton, 1st Baron, 121
Adam, 113
Addiction, 8, 49, 106
   to Internet, 8
Aeschylus, v, vi, 131
Alcohol, 38, 64
Alienation, 71, 106
Altruistic, 27, 108
Antipsychotic medication, 65, 66
Antisocial personalities, 79
Anxiety, 4, 8, 20, 49, 50, 70, 71, 77, 89, 93, 101, 108, 124, 125, 127
Appetite, 72
Archimedes, 11, 12
Arguments, 32, 41, 57–59, 100
Aristotle, 9
Asking for help, 10
al-Assad, Bashar, 119
Associative memory system, 13
Atomistic thinking, 86
Audit of Improvement, 78
Authentizotic organizations, 102
Authoritarianism, 100
Authority, 84, 88, 117, 126
Autocratic leaders, 101
Autonomy, 100, 102

B

Bad habits, 8, 9, 28
Becket, Samuel, 19
Belligerent personalities, 55–59
Belonging, 4, 120
Benzene, 12
Biden, Joseph, 125, 126
Births, 92
Blood pressure, 82
Bloomberg, 48
Bluebeard, 111–114
Body language, 76, 78
Bolsonaro, Jair, 119
Borderline personalities, 63
Bowlby, John, 92

Index

Brain
  complaining and, 52
  dopamine, 14, 31
  mass hysteria and, 124, 125, 127, 128
  psychosis and, 64
  sleep and, 12, 13
  time perception and, 31–32
Brazil, 119
Bridget Jones's Diary (Fielding), 37
Bruegel the Younger, 123
Bullying, 116

C

Cabin fever, 19
Campbell, Joseph, viii
Cancer, 71, 84
Candide (Voltaire), 129, 130
Career coaches, 94
Champion, David, viii
Chaucer, Geoffrey, 19
Cheak-Baillargeon, Alicia, viii
Chesterton, Gilbert Keith, 55
Childhood
  belligerent personality and, 55–59, 108
  dissociative identity disorder and, 48
  loneliness and, 108
  relationships and, 3, 76
  time perception and, 30
Chimpanzees, 101
Churchill, Winston, 99
Cinderella, 111
Cleese, John, 14
Cognitive decline, 107
Cognitive illusions, 32, 33
Co-housing communities, 108
Co-leadership, 85–89
Collaboration, 16, 88, 115, 127
Command-and-control systems, 100
Communication, 8, 17, 40–41, 53, 72, 89

Community, 5, 83, 94, 99, 101, 106–108
Company cultures, 87
Compartmentalization, 49, 50
Compassion, 26, 78
Competence, 4, 5
Complaining, 63
Confucius, 91
Confusion, 50, 87, 89, 102
Conrad, Joseph, 105
Consensus-building, 100
Conspiracy theories, 116, 117, 127, 128
Control, 4, 5, 9, 20, 22–24, 26, 28, 38, 41, 49, 53, 56, 58, 64, 65, 77, 92, 100, 112, 114, 130, 131
Conversational judo, 58
Core values, 39, 87
Corporate authoritarianism, 100
Corporate democracy, 100
Count of Monte Cristo, The (Dumas), 15, 16
Coup de foudre, 36
Covid-19 pandemic
  forgetfulness and, 29
  groundhog days and, 25–28
  leaders and, 25, 115, 117, 127, 128
  loneliness and, 107
  time perception and, 30, 32
Crazy ideas, 36, 57, 67, 70, 73, 76, 82, 116, 127
Creative endeavors, 8
Creativity, 12, 14, 26, 39, 102
Critical thinking, 121
Crusades, 124
Cults, 25, 125, 126

D

Daily hassles patience, 20
Dalai Lama, 131
Dancing plagues, 124, 126
David (Michelangelo), 13

Daydreams, 22
Death, 4, 19, 92, 93, 107, 111–113, 124, 125
Decision-making processes, 85, 87, 99, 100
Defense mechanisms, 49, 50, 59, 64, 125
Defensive postures, 77
Demagoguery, 128
Dementia, 107
Democracy, 99–103
Denial, 70, 72, 117
Dependency reactions, 101, 120
Depression
   energy barometer and, 7–10
   groundhog days and, 27
   retirement and, 91–96
   revenge and, 17
   shadow self and, 48–50
De Waal, Frans, 123
Dictatorship, 102
Disengagement, 81
Disraeli, Benjamin, 51, 81
Dissociative identity disorder, 48
Division of labor, 42
Divorce, 92, 107
Don't rock the boat, 82
Dopamine, 14, 31
Dualities, 86
Dumas, Alexandre, 15, 16
Duterte, Rodrigo, 119
Dyadic structures, 85

Eating habits, 8, 72
Eco-therapy, 33
Education, 12, 87, 114, 128, 131
Effectiveness, 78, 82, 102
Einstein, Albert, 14
Empathy, 8, 22, 26, 56, 59, 78, 79, 116, 120
Energy barometer, 7–10

Engagement, 14, 41, 82, 100, 102, 103
Engellau, Elisabet, viii
Erdoğan, Recep Tayyip, 119
Erikson, Erik, 47, 69
Eudaimonia, 9
Eureka moments, 11–14
European Union, 128
Eve, 113
Evolution, 124
Exercise, 8, 17, 22, 30, 53, 89, 94, 107
Experimenters, 93
Experts, 127, 128
Exploration, 102
Eye for an eye, 15

Facebook, 106
FaceTime, 61, 62
Fact-based society, 128
Failures, 49, 70, 84, 89, 94
Fair process, 83, 102
Fairy tales, 111–113
False personas, 77
Family, 3, 8, 9, 14, 20, 24, 27, 29, 37, 50, 53, 55, 56, 61–66, 71, 72, 86, 94, 106, 107
Fantasizing, 18
Feedback, viii, 58, 82, 84, 89, 117
Financial planning, 94
Firing people, 78
Five pillars of meaning, 3–6
Flattery, 75, 78, 116
Flight or flight response, 20, 124
Ford, Henry, 85
Forgetfulness, 29–33
Forgiveness, 18, 40
Frankl, Victor, 4
Franklin, Benjamin, 99
Free speech, 128
Freud, Sigmund, 25, 61, 119
Friedman, Thomas, 127
Fromm, Erich, 116

Functional magnetic resonance imaging (fMRI), 13
Futurists, 106

G

Gallup poll, 100
Gandhi, Mohandas "Mahatma," 50
Garbage cans, 9, 52
Garner, John, 115
Genital mutilation, 114
Gibran, Kahlil, 96
Global warming, 127, 131
Goethe, Johann Wolfgang von, 51
Good cop/bad cop, 86
Grandparenting, 93
Gratitude, 23, 52, 54
Greater negative affect, 17
Grief, vi, 92
Groundhog Day (1993 film), 26–28
Groupthink, 124–128
Growing together, 41–43
Gut feelings, 76, 78

H

Habits, vi, 8, 9, 28, 52, 54, 72
Harvard Business Review, viii
Harvard Longitudinal Study, 94
Hedonia, 9
Helplessness, feelings of, 131
Hesse, Herman, 6
Hidden agendas, 76–79
Hierarchy, 84, 101
High-trust cultures, 84
Histoires ou contes du temps passé (Perrault), 111
Histrionic personalities, 56
Hitler, Adolf, 126
Hoffer, Erik, v
Homer, 29
Honesty, 89
Human resources, 94

Humor, 23, 42
Humpty-Dumpty, 127
Hungary, 119, 126
Hunger, 131
Hurry sickness, 8

I

Impatience, 20–24
Incubation, 12, 13
India, 119
Individual space, 41
Individuation, 65
INSEAD, v, viii, 3, 8, 76
Insomnia, 7, 107
Instagram, 106
Instant gratification, 20
Intergenerational solidarity, 106
Internet addiction, 8
Interpersonal measures, 87–89
Interpersonal patience, 20
Interpersonal relationships, 3, 4, 56
Intervention plans, 25
Intimacy, 26, 36, 40, 106
Intuition, 76
Italy, 27

J

Johnson, Alexander Boris, 126
Johnson, Samuel, 35, 81
Judicial independence, 99, 121
Jung, Carl, 48, 49

K

Keith, Arthur, 55
Kekulé, August, 12
Khashoggi, Jamal, 119
King of Hearts (1966 film), 73
Kipling, Rudyard, 128
Know thyself, 36, 88, 131
Kool-Aid, drinking of, 123–128

L

La Bruyère, Jean de, 29
Lao Tzu, 83
Laporte, Isabelle, viii
Laughing, 23
Leaders, 25, 76, 86, 89, 101, 102, 117, 120, 121, 125–128, 131
Lex talionis, 15
Life-changing events, 92
Life hardship patience, 20
Logarithmic scales, 32
Loneliness, 37, 67, 71, 76, 95
Lotus-eaters, 29
Love, 28, 36, 42
   at first sight, 36

M

Maladaptive social cognition, 108
Malignant narcissists, 115–117, 120
Mandela, Nelson, 132
Manic defense, 9, 14
Mao Zedong, 126
Marcus Aurelius, Roman Emperor, 18
Marriage, 47, 106, 111, 112
Mass hysteria, 124–128
McCartney, Paul, 12
Meditation, 13, 33
Mentoring, 95
Michelangelo, 13
Mindfulness, 24
Mission, 73, 75, 83, 87
Mistakes, 9, 26, 38, 40, 82, 84
Mixed-age residences, 108
Modi, Narendra, 119
Mohammed Bin Salman, Prince, 119
Mood changes, 71
Moral panics, 124
Movies, 8, 16, 25–27, 130
Murder, 101, 111, 113, 119
Mutual respect, 39
"My way or the highway" approach, 89

N

Narcissism, 116
Nation state, 99, 115
Nature, exposure to, 8, 33
Negative people, 9
Negativity, 51, 52, 54
Neophilia/phobia, 33
Netherlands, 27
New York Times, The, 127
Nietzsche, Friedrich, 35, 61
Niksen, 13, 106
Nilsson, Harry, 105
Non-rapid eye movement (NREM) sleep, 12
Novelty, 31–33, 36
Nuclear weapons, 131

O

Odyssey, The (Homer), 29
Offboarding, 92–95
Office gossip, 84
Onboarding, 84, 91–96
Orbán, Viktor, 119
Organizational socialization, *see* Onboarding
Overpopulation, 131
Oxytocin, 22

P

Palaeolithic era, 16
Paranoia, 64, 81, 82, 120, 127
Parenting, 25, 88
Part-time roles, 92
Pascal, Blaise, 75
Patience, 19–24
Perfectionism, 9
Performance appraisals, 82
Perrault, Charles, 111–113
Personality profiles, 17
Pessimism, v
Pets, 108

Philippines, 119, 126
Physical attractiveness, 36
Poland, 126
Polarization, 116
Politics, 48, 99, 126
Portfolio careers, 92
Poverty of the self, 106
Press freedom, 99
Procreation, 42, 101
Productivity, 70, 71, 83, 100
Profitability, 63, 83
Profit with purpose, 102
Projective identification, 52
Prosocial behavior, 23
Prostitution, 114
Protest, despair, and detachment, 92, 94
Psychic epidemics, 123, 124
Psychoanalysis, 52, 112
Psychopathic personalities, 17, 116
Psychosis, 64
Psychotherapy, 65, 72, 108
Public recognition, 84
Purpose, 4, 5, 27, 28, 33, 54, 76, 77, 83, 93, 102, 108, 113
Purposeless, 13, 54
Putin, Vladimir, 119

Rape, 114, 129
Rapid eye movement (REM) sleep, 12, 13
Rationalization, 49, 50
Reading, viii, 8, 129
Reflectivity, 124
Reframing, 22
Regression, 117, 120
Rejection, fear of, 77
Republican Party, 48
Retirement, 91–96
Revenge, 15–18
Richness of the self, 106

Robertson, James, 92
Role definition, 87
Roosevelt, Franklin, v
Rousseau, Jean-Jacques, 19
Rule of law, 119, 128
Rumi, 115
Russell, Bertrand, 102
Russia, 119

Safe spaces, 89
Satanism, 124
Saudi Arabia, 119
Saviors, 101, 120
Schizophrenia, 70
Schweitzer, Albert, 105
Self-actualization, 102
Self-confidence, 59, 131
Self-deception, 50
Self-efficacy, 5, 59
Self-esteem, 16, 57
Selfishness, 26
Self-medication, 8
Self-reflection, 25, 33, 94
Self-sacrifice, 10, 38
Seneca, 3
Separation, vi, 92, 121
Serenity Prayer, 23
Sex, 9, 36, 112
Shadow self, 48–50
Shakespeare, William, 35
Slavery, 114
Sleep, 11–13, 63
Sleeping Beauty, 111
Slogans, 121, 125
Social media, 106, 125–128
Societal regression, 120
Soft skills, 84, 88
Solitude, vii, 14, 33, 37, 105, 106, 109
Space, 14, 26, 41, 66, 89, 102, 106, 108
Splitting, 64, 76, 79, 125

Stalin, Josef, 126
Steadfast people, 93
Strengths and weaknesses, 36, 88
Stress, vii, 8, 20, 22, 25, 27, 51, 53, 73, 83, 86, 92, 93, 100, 107
Structural measures, 87–88
Substance abuse, 47, 70, 72
Suggestibility, 124
Suicide, 69, 70
Sympathy, seeking of, 53
Synergies, 86
Syria, 119

Teaching, 21, 95, 130
Team dynamics, 11, 83
Technology, 106
Terrorism, 131
Thatcher, Margaret, 111
Thoreau, Henry David, 69
Three Bs, 12
Time perception, 30–32
Tipping points, 27
Trance states, 123
Transcendence, 4, 5
Transparency, 64, 70, 83
Truman, Harry, 85
Trump, Donald, 119, 125, 126, 128
Trust
   belligerent personalities and, 56
   borderline personalities and, 63
   co-leadership and, 89
   depression and, 117
   hidden agendas and, 78
   organizations and, 77, 78, 81–84
   politics and, 117
   relationships and, 40, 82, 89
Tulip mania, 124
Turkey, 119, 126
Turtle symbolism, vi
Twain, Mark, 7

Unconscious mind, 11, 13, 14
Unemployment, 106
Unfinished psychological business, 38
United Kingdom (UK), 126
United States (US)
   loneliness in, 107
   mental disorders in, 70
   Trump administration, 119
Us *vs.* them, 79, 120, 125

Victimhood, 16, 17, 27, 53, 55, 56, 124, 125
Virginity, 112
Vision, 31, 66, 87, 91, 102, 123, 131
Visualization, 22
Vitus, Saint, 123, 124
Voltaire, 129, 130
Voluntary work, 93–95

Waiting for Godot (Becket), 19
War, 55, 73, 131
Wifely obedience, 114
Wilde, Oscar, 35, 75
Witch hunts, 124
Women, 4, 111–114, 130
Workaholism, 3
Working from home, 106
World Health Organization (WHO), 70
Writing, vii, viii, 33

Yeats, William Butler, 111
"Yesterday" (The Beatles), 12

Zootikos, 102

Ingram Content Group UK Ltd.
Milton Keynes UK
UKHW020142050723
424579UK00004B/373